What to Read in The Rain

The Greater Seattle Bureau of Fearless Ideas
8414 Greenwood Ave. N.
Seattle, Washington 98103
www.fearlessideas.org
206-725-2625

Editor: Bill Thorness
Designer: Tony Ong
Printer: Consolidated Press, Seattle
Special thanks to Amazon.com for helping fund this project.

ISBN 978-0-9886038-1-3

What to
Read in The

RAIN

Writing from
**THE GREATER SEATTLE BUREAU
OF FEARLESS IDEAS**
by famous and not-yet-famous
adult and young writers

The Greater Seattle Bureau of Fearless Ideas is a neighborhood center that encourages fearless creativity among our youth while teaching them the essential skill of writing. One must be fearless to write well! Tell the truth! Be exact in those details! Stand tall! Show your colors! (We also—while we're on the topic—encourage fearless compassion, empathy, and kindness.) To encourage all of this work, we match young people with trained adult mentors who help them with inspiration, grammar, and punctuation—mentors who themselves are writing their stories and sharing them, not to mention being kind and empathetic.

At the Bureau we believe that if you write your stories well and share those stories proudly, and can listen to others' stories with the same attentiveness and interest that you want them to listen to your stories, well, there will be a whole lot of learning going on. Your stories will change if you are listening to my stories…and vice versa. And you will understand me better…and vice versa.

And the world will be a better place.

What a fearless idea.

Table of Contents

TERI HEIN is the founding Executive Director of The Greater Seattle Bureau of Fearless Ideas, a writing center formerly known as 826 Seattle. Under that name, with the help of hundreds of trained volunteers, the organization inspired thousands of children to perfect the art and skill of writing. Our new name, The Greater Seattle Bureau of Fearless Ideas, reflects our plan to forge forward into all forms of communication … with the same grace, excellence, and humor. Same staff. Same board. Same volunteers. Same students. Same great vibes. Prior to getting the fearless idea of starting the organization, Teri taught for many years and did a fair amount of writing, including her award-winning memoir *Atomic Farmgirl*.

Introduction

You are holding in your hands a rather fearless idea brought to you, not surprisingly, by The Greater Seattle Bureau of Fearless Ideas[1], a neighborhood youth writing center located in the Greenwood neighborhood of Seattle.

Here is the fearless idea we had back in 2010: Could we ask well known, immensely talented Northwest authors to donate an excellent piece of writing for an anthology? Meanwhile we would keep doing what we do so well: inspire and teach young people to write their stories. We would then work one-on-one with these students to perfect their writing so we could publish their stories alongside the adult authors' stories in a world-class book of writing that celebrates the literary talent of the Pacific Northwest. Once this collection was in print, we would have an excellent compilation to sell in bookstores, as the makers of books do.

But an even more fearless idea occurred to us: we could also partner with hotels in Seattle who would place the books bedside for the reading enjoyment of their guests.

Hotel guests would be immediately drawn to the book[2] and, with our invitation to purchase, claim it as a souvenir to add to their libraries at home or as a gift for a loved one.

What a crazy idea, right? No famous author would donate a story, even to a worthy cause like a youth writing center! No child can write stories that are of interest to strangers! No luxury hotel would purchase cases of such a book to place in every room!

Wrong. You hold in your hand the fifth edition of *What to Read in the Rain*. Since 2011, thousands of copies of this book have been purchased by hotel guests and other literature lovers and flown off to all parts of the world. We have received postcards from Qatar, Sweden, and Madison, Wisconsin! Yes! People love this project.

Writing *is* a fearless endeavor, so thank you so much for your support of The Greater Seattle Bureau of Fearless Ideas, an organization that strives to inspire young people to write and then helps them to write their stories well. And now: enjoy.

[1] *If you are a collector of these editions—this is the 5th— until very recently we were known as 826 Seattle, which was a perfectly worthy name but didn't accurately reflect our fearlessness.*

[2] *Studies have shown that luxury hotel guests consume an above-average amount of excellent literature.*

TOM ROBBINS is a board member of The Greater Seattle Bureau of Fearless Ideas and author of nine novels, including *Fierce Invalids Home from Hot Climates* and *Villa Incognito*, a collection of short stories, and the recently published memoir, *Tibetan Peach Pie.*

The Importance of Being Envious

At the onset, I have to state that I'm not convinced that there's any such thing as "writer's block." I suspect that what we like to call "writer's block" is in fact a failure of nerve or a failure of imagination or both.

If you're willing to break rules, risk ridicule, and explore the unknown, and if you've somehow managed, despite social conditioning, to hold on to your imagination (more's the pity of you haven't), then you can dissolve any so-called block simply by imagining extraordinary, heretofore unthinkable solutions, and/or by playing around uninhibitedly with language. It's quite possible to imagine or wordplay, conjure or sport your way out of any impasse.

Prolonged neurotic blockages aside, however, it would be false not to acknowledge that every working writer experiences days when the ideas and images reveal themselves more reluctantly than usual. Biorhythms could be at fault, it could be a savage hangover, external or internal distractions, or one of those ruptures that occur periodically in the pipeline from the Other. (Writing imaginative fiction is such a mysterious enterprise that often there's no way to explain its sources except to attribute them to Something Out There Somewhere.)

On those dreaded occasions when your muse shambles in wearing army boots, it may be time to tap into one of the strongest and most persistent, if seldom discussed, human emotions: *jealousy.*

Yes, we should never underestimate the valuable role that sheer envy plays in the creative process. Whereas in a romantic relationship jealousy is stupid and destructive, as a lubricant of the verbal brain machinery it can be highly effective. It's elementary: you read a few pages (sometimes a few paragraphs or even a line or two will suffice) of work of which you are in awe, and in minutes you'll find yourself motivated—burning!—to try to compose passages of equal merit.

Well, at least envy can usually motivate *me*. On a pedestrian morning, grounded in a no-fly zone without a banjo on my knee, I'll read, say, a poem by Pablo Neruda or César Vallejo, turn to the early pages of Anaïs Nin's *Seduction of the Minotaur*, sample a bit of Pynchon, Nabokov or Henry Miller; or even dial up Bob Dylan on the iPod, and soon I've waxed six shades of pistachio and kiwi. The green beast has awakened and is starting to chase me down the street.

Call it forced inspiration if you will, call it literary Viagra, but as a writing exercise, envy works. "Could I not coin phrases that smoke and pop like those do?" I'll ask. "Is that guy's word-bag really that much bigger than mine?" Or, "Do I have the gust to work as close to the bull as she does?" Feeling almost ashamed in the presence of such verve, I'll return to my idling narrative primed to redeem—and entertain—myself.

By no means is this a case of competing for fortune or fame. It isn't as if I want to elbow Salman Rushdie out of line at the bank or steal Louise Erdrich's magical ink. What I desire is to feel for myself the *rush* Salman or Louise must have felt when they pulled that particular rabbit out of a hat. What I covet is to have the kind of effect on language-conscious readers that Rushdie and Erdrich have just had on me.

Ultimately, it doesn't matter whether your prose actually meets the master's unintentional challenge. That degree of success is probably not in your cards. But you have to believe it might be. And in merely attempting, with every muscle in your envious psyche, to climb to that elevation—to be that inventive and amusing and tough and daring and true—you may well have mooned the drab angel of mediocrity, and if nothing else, you will have let loose your juice.

CHELSEA CAIN is the author of *The New York Times* bestselling Archie Sheridan thriller series, including *Heartsick, Sweetheart, Evil at Heart, The Night Season, Kill You Twice,* and *Let Me Go*. Her Portland-based thrillers have been published in over 30 languages, recommended on "The Today Show," and have appeared in episodes of HBO's "True Blood" and ABC's "Castle." Stephen King included two of her books in his top ten favorite books of the year, and NPR named *Heartsick* one of the best 100 thrillers ever written. Chelsea's new book *One Kick* (Simon & Schuster, 2014) launches the Kick Lannigan series.

For Your Safety:

A Guide to Serial Killers, Bears, Sneaker Waves and Other Attractions of the Pacific Northwest

Greetings! Welcome to the Pacific Northwest. As you probably noticed on your way to the hotel, this is a pretty spectacular region. (If it was raining, come back in August when the cloud cover has lifted enough for you to see what I'm talking about. Seriously, there are mountains on the horizon. We hear about them all the time.) Most likely you already know a bit about the area. If not, I'm sure that you can find an interesting array of reading material about local restaurants and attractions fanned out neatly on the desk in your hotel room. But there is more going on here than coffee, locally sourced cuisine, rock bands, multinational software companies and epidemic levels of vitamin D deficiency. Please take a minute to go over the following items that may come up during your stay.

SERIAL KILLERS I don't mean to alarm you. Your hotel is perfectly safe. It is run by decent, security-minded people. Any place with a classy anthology like this in the room is going to have quality down pillows, really nice conditioner, and excellent locks on the doors. I am certain that a housekeeper has already checked under your bed. Also, no offense, but serial killers, studies tell us, prefer to kill locals rather than tourists. (I think this is because you tend to stay away from dive bars.) See. You are not in any danger. Still, you should know that the Pacific Northwest has produced an impressive array of psychopaths. For a while, when Ted Bundy was active in Seattle in the early seventies, we were losing a female college student with long dark hair parted down the middle at an average of one per month. Then there was the Green River Killer. I was ten when they found the first three victims of the Green River Killer. I was thirty when they finally caught him. His name was Gary Ridgway and he pled guilty to murdering forty-eight women, making him the most prolific serial killer in U.S. history. Heard of him? Unless you're a local, you probably haven't. He has a really bad publicist. And then there were the

Hillside Stranglers, one of whom worked at the store in Bellingham, Washington, where I bought my back-to-school clothes every year. Up in Vancouver, B.C., a pig farmer was convicted of killing six women. But they're pretty confident that the real number is closer to forty-nine. Being a pig farmer provided an excellent way to dispose of bodies, if you know what I mean. And that's just the tip of the iceberg. But do not fret! There are some simple precautions you can take to avoid these local predators.

1. Do not engage in prostitution.
2. Avoid being a Caucasian.
3. Avoid being a female.
4. Avoid being between twenty and forty years old.
5. Stay out of vans.

NATURAL DISASTERS YOU MAY ENCOUNTER DURING YOUR STAY:

EARTHQUAKES The Pacific Northwest sits on the Cascadia Subduction Zone, a fault that runs parallel to the Pacific coast of North America, from northern California to Vancouver Island. You've heard of the "big one" that they're expecting in California? Well they call this the "bigger one," and it's basically expected any minute. No worries! You're staying at a hotel. Someone has already thought about this for you. There is a little map on the back of your door showing the path you should take out of the building. Plus, you've got fire extinguishers at your disposal. Why I bet there's even a generator. Just be sure to go over a reunion plan with your family and remember, "Drop, cover, hold on."

TSUNAMIS If you're staying at the Pacific coast you will want to take a brief gander at the best route to high ground. Just look for the signs with the picture of a cute little tsunami on them. Also, if you hear what sounds like an air raid siren during any point of your stay, or if you look out and notice that the ocean seems to have "gone away," this would be a very good time to run like hell. The nice people at your hotel can point you in the right direction.

ADDITIONAL MISCELLANEOUS DANGERS THAT MAY CAUSE YOU GRAVE BODILY HARM:

SNEAKER WAVES I can't tell you how many tourists we lose to these things, so pay attention. Do not turn your back on the ocean. You know those huge waves you see crashing onto the sand? Every once in a while an even huger wave will crash onto the shore. These are called sneaker waves because they tend to surprise the people they crash down on and pull out to sea and drown. Since people usually turn their backs on the ocean to pose for a picture, this can result in entire wedding parties being sucked into the Pacific in front of horrified wedding photographers. No one wants to see those pictures, so the photographer doesn't get paid. This is bad for the local economy.

KILLER LOGS Sometimes the ocean coughs a log up onto the beach. Kids love to play on these logs. Here's the thing—it just take a few inches of water seeping under that log for it to roll over on top of the child and suddenly it's not so fun anymore. The tide is coming in and your kid is pinned under a log, and once that log is on top of a child, it is very hard to get off. Do not cavort on shoreline timber.

AMATEUR MUSHROOM HUNTING Every year someone goes out into the woods with a few printouts from the Internet, intent on harvesting fungi. If you are a fan of exotic mushrooms, the concierge can direct you to the proper farmer's market. Do not go mushroom hunting. This only leads to poison control getting involved and can make the trip a real bummer for you and your family.

THE HELICOPTER OR SMALL PLANE "LAW OF GENERATIONS" Occasionally visitors will hire a small plane or helicopter to take them on a scenic tour. By all means, enjoy the view. Just be aware of the helicopter or small plane "law of generations," which states that the chance of crashing increases exponentially along with the number of generations of a family onboard. Never ever fly with four or more generations. These flights almost always crash.

VITAMIN D DEFICIENCY Due to the lack of sun exposure, we get very little Vitamin D out here, so you will want to take a supplement during your stay. Even if it appears that the sun is out during your visit, the local population is so sun-starved that we tend to soak up all the available benefit.

SUICIDE Your risk of suicide increases every day you stay in the Northwest.* Be aware of changes in mood. If any member of your family starts giving away personal items or writing sad emo songs, you might consider moving your departure date up.

MORE WAYS TREES CAN KILL YOU I've already mentioned the Killer Logs. Trees also kill snowboarders and skiers at an alarming rate—they seem to jump right out in front of them as they're careening down the mountain. It's fair; we've cut a lot of trees down, so they are taking us all out one by one. Still, we don't have to make it easy for them. If you must strap your feet to a board and slide down a mountainside, wear a helmet. Do not approach a tree after a windstorm or ice storm—it might throw a hundred pound branch at you. If a bear attacks you during your visit (more on that in a moment), do not climb a tree. This is a piece of misinformation spread by trees in an effort to make us look foolish. Bears are quite adept at climbing.

BEAR ATTACKS Here's the trick: The proper response depends on what type of bear you are facing.

BLACK BEAR If you see a black bear, and he does not see you, slip quietly away and start constructing a nice story you can tell back home. If he sees you, stay calm and "identify yourself as human." This involves standing up and waving your arms over your head. Do not say the word "bear." (As in, "Please, Bear, do not eat me.") The black bear may associate the word "bear" with food and come trotting over. (People sometimes feed wild bears, calling out, "Here, Bear!" every time they toss them a snack. This has created some confusion for bears, who now believe that the word "bear" means "Dinnertime! Come and get it!")** If identifying yourself doesn't work, try to scare the bear by clapping your hands, looking the bear in the eye, and generally being dickish. This usually does the trick. If not, then make a run for it. Again, do not climb a tree. The bear and the tree will laugh at you, and then the bear will eat you in front of your family.

GRIZZLY BEAR So, basically the opposite of everything I've just said applies here. If you happen to run into a Grizzly during your visit, avoid direct eye contact. Stay very calm and quiet. Identify yourself as human by waving your arms, but do it in a serene fashion and speak only in a low, monotonous voice, sort of like you're trying to get the attention of a snotty server at a high end restaurant filled with elderly diners. If this doesn't work, then curl up into a ball and try to survive the attack. Never run. Never act aggressive. Even if the bear is charging at you, remain still and try to go to your calm place. Grizzlies love to bluff. They will charge right at you, get within a couple of feet, and then lope off chuckling.

RAVINES If one of your traveling companions should vanish while driving in the Northwest, it is almost certain that this person has crashed into a ravine and is trapped in the vehicle out of sight from the road. We are always finding people in cars at the bottom of ravines. Some of these ravines have thirty or forty cars in them, with bodies dating back to the forties. Always check local ravines when you are missing a loved one.

MUDSLIDES Do not enter a stilt house during a rainstorm.

JAPANESE TSUNAMI DEBRIS If you come across tsunami debris while beachcombing, it's probably not radioactive, but just in case, cover your reproductive organs and back away.

OTHER ITEMS OF POTENTIAL INTEREST FOR TRAVELERS:

Do not carry an umbrella. Nothing says, "Not from around here," like a person carrying an umbrella in the Northwest. It just isn't done. It rains here all the time. You are going to get wet. Deal with it. We have given up. If you are concerned, do what we do and wear something with a hood.

Cyclists always have the right of way. (They don't really, but they will yell at you if you don't give it to them.)

If it gets above 55 degrees and the sun is out, dress like it's 85. Anything above 54 is shorts weather as far as we're concerned. We don't see the sun that often, and when we do we like to take advantage of it.

Washington State has a lot of speed traps along I-5. Oregon does not.

Almost everyone you meet in Seattle will work at Microsoft. This can be confusing. How can so many people work for one company? Are some of them lying? No. Microsoft just has a really big campus.

Food carts are different here. They're not the taco trucks that pull up at construction sights in other parts of the country. Our food trucks serve crepes and Belgian truffle fries with bone marrow aioli.

The word "beach" can be a bit misleading to out-of-towners. Don't show up at a Northwest beach with a swimsuit and a bottle of Coppertone. Instead think: Polar Fleece. It is always at least ten degrees colder at the beach than wherever you are when you load up the car. You can also count on forty-knot winds and high surf. For much of the year, add sideways rain to that equation. We do not swim in this water. We look at it through the windows of our beach houses.

All the men have facial hair here. No one knows why. They just all grew beards a few years ago. Styles range from the full lumberjack to the waxed mustache. If you have time to grow muttonchops before your next trip, I would recommend it. You will probably get better service at the food carts.

A FINAL THOUGHT:

Please think twice before you move here. Sometimes when people visit, the next thing we know they have sold everything and have moved here to open a bookstore, start a band, or open a bicycle repair shop. We appreciate your interest and enthusiasm—but we have enough of these things. We also have enough cycle powered smoothie places, pedicabs, and microbreweries. If you must start a business here, I suggest podiatry or opening a nice mustache wax store. If you have only visited in August or September, please be aware that it is totally unlike that here the entire rest of the year.

You're totally going to move here, aren't you?

That's fine. You seem nice. You clearly have excellent taste in hotels and reading material. Just do me a favor, okay? When you go home to pack up the house, tell your friends how dangerous it is here.

Tell them you barely made it out alive.

In the meantime, I hope you find this information useful. Thank you for visiting, and enjoy your stay.

Perhaps related to the Vitamin D deficiency.
**Do not feed wild bears.*

JESS WALTER is the author of eight books, including the #1 *New York Times* bestseller *Beautiful Ruins*. He was a finalist for the 2006 National Book Award for *The Zero* and won the 2005 Edgar Allan Poe award for *Citizen Vince*. He's been a finalist for the *L.A. Times* Book Prize and the PEN/USA Literary Prize in both fiction and nonfiction, and twice has won the Pacific Northwest Booksellers Award. His most recent book, the short story collection, *We Live in Water*, was long-listed for the Story Prize and the Frank O'Connor International Story Prize. His books have been translated in 30 languages and his short fiction has appeared in *Best American Short Stories, Harpers, McSweeney's, Esquire* and elsewhere. He lives with his family in Spokane, Washington.

Song of Spokane

Our voices cried (*We will ...*)
north side to South Hill
Wandermere, Qualchan and Manito
(We will only ...) from Luna to Rancho Chico
and while test-driving a high-miles Chrysler
at the East Sprague Cheap Wheels
(We will only be ...) sipping tea
at the service desk of Liberty Lake Mercedes
(We will only be happy ...) at 24-hour Fitness
open all night for when the paradox hits us
that for all our talk of sustainability
the only way to avoid obesity
is to work off all these calories
on treadmills with our own private TVs.

(We will only be happy when ...)
we confide to therapists in clinics and HMOs
We will only be happy when we get a Trader Joe's.
(They have them in Seattle, you know.)

And on the day that ours opened
the therapists' eyes were bleary
from nights without sleep
as they made appointments to see

their own listless shrinks
and confess their deep-seated fear
that a whole city's sadness might disappear
when the lights came on at the Joe's here
It would be awful, the frightened therapists agreed,
if a new grocery store actually made us all ... happy.

But not to worry.
No-one ever went broke in America—
in the unhappiness business ...

And so even two-buck chuck
isn't nearly enough
to relieve the stuff
that collects on our dissatisfied parietal lobes
like January snow
I remember one from a few years ago
that caused all the streets to close
and the schools to shut down
and the sudden realization that perhaps in a town
of two hundred thousand
we might want to invest
... in a second plow.

But what I really remember
is my son and I building a snow fort
and having the county assess it
as worth more than our home
and how nice it all was
how peaceful and quiet
we couldn't even leave home
if we'd wanted to try it
let alone go for a chub of smoked gouda at Trader Joe's
which, flash to the day that it opened
was filled with those sleepless red-eyed therapists
thinking (*Now we will* ....)
as they looked at their own shopping lists

—pasta, potstickers and a dry Gewürztraminer—
and as the real poet said, "Let be be finale of seem" … er

Maybe not.
Maybe the answer does lie
in a hand-crafted beer
And an apple-pecan pie
Which is why we ply those aisles with hunger and fear
as the voices cry (*Now we will …*) and you can hear
them pleading, from Ferris to Mead, LC to CV
(Now we will only be …)
flooding this river valley with our restless moods.
Now we will only be happy when we get a Whole Foods.

And maybe it's not so crazy to imagine
salvation's pathway so fine and narrow
that they only sell it at Crate and Barrel
or that true joy awaits and fulfillment arrives
in aisles of organic beets and endives
(and honestly I don't even know what an endive is
but I thought it sounded like arrive
and I see them on menus sometimes
but maybe I'm working too hard here to rhyme)
which reminds me that what I drive
is not my wife's Toyota Prius
but a 1963 Continental by Lincoln
in that most American of hues
the orange of prison jump suits
six thousand pounds of steel uni-body engineering
that gets nine miles to the gallon of premium
and I often feel the disapproval
of enviro-lefties like yours truly
thinking, *Don't you care about the world that you leave behind?*

You know.

For the children?

And that's when I have to force myself to recall
just how crappy other people's children are
like this little shit who sat next to me
on a three hour flight from Denver to eternity
this crazy lap child who kicked and fussed
and thrashed about wildly while his poor mom hushed
him and the rest of us recalled that movie
about the plane crash in the Andes
as the Mom gave Damien a Red Bull and some candy
and we wondered if a forty-minute delay was enough justification
to become cannibals—because there'd be no hesitation
about who to eat first … and that's when
Damien's mom smiled at me and said, *He usually travels so easily*
and with that Damien's head spun 360 degrees
and he delivered a roundhouse kick to my teeth
as flames shot out of his little shit eyes
and the mom said, *Honey, what's the matter with you tonight?*
and this monster kid looked up at me
and like some genius existential prodigy
in the voice of all humanity, he said: *I'm! Not! Happy!*

And us? What about us?
Will we ever be happy? I have no idea—
but I suspect that one day we will
when we finally get an Ikea.

Adventures From Afar

Good writing takes a reader on a journey. The stories in this section take that responsibility literally. The adventure stories in this section come from a vast variety of sources—a Viking-saga themed writing workshop, a daily journal of creative musings, and a botany-themed summer writing class, to name a few. Despite their different themes and locations, each story uses narrative to take the reader to a new and unexplored world.

YUSUF ALI-HALANE is seventeen and lives in Burien. He is an extremely talented writer who has been featured in a number of publications at The Greater Seattle Bureau of Fearless Ideas.

In Search of the Next Sherlock Holmes

As a child, I had always admired the Wright Brothers. The fact that two men managed to invent and fly the world's first successful airplane was absolutely jaw-dropping. I would often find myself dreaming that I was there on that cold December day nearly sixty-two years ago during the event. I mean, the thought of being able to fly was something most (if not all) of us would love to be able to do. Who would've thought that I would one day be on a Boeing 707 heading for England? I certainly didn't, until my boss at *The New York Times* called me into his office on a cold December morning.

"How can I help you, sir?" I asked in a confused tone. The room was musty and dimly lit. His desk was cluttered with potential stories and his walls covered with awards.

"John, how would you feel about going to the other side of the Atlantic?"

"I'm not sure, sir. Why?"

"Several sources indicate that London's most famous mystery writer is planning on hanging it all up for good. They say he could be the next Sir Arthur Conan Doyle."

"Doyle? You mean guy who wrote the Sherlock Holmes series?"

"That's the one. So you can see how promising this new writer could be. I need you to take a plane to London to figure out what exactly is going on."

"Of course!" I exclaimed. It wasn't the story that had gotten me excited; it was the fact that I was going to ride inside a plane for the first time ever. Call me a little kid, but the thought of flying is an amazing thing. Even at the age of twenty-three, I still dreamed that I was flying in the air as if I were Superman.

Of course I agreed to the job, and just like that I found myself walking towards the Boeing 707 that would carry me and several other people across the Atlantic and into London, the heart of England.

I stopped halfway there and just stood on the runway gazing at this beautiful piece of art. Yeah, it can be viewed as "just a hunk of metal." But it's so much more than that; it's a symbol of progress, innovation, and promise. As humans, we've come from walking on our own two feet to flying in the air. And if we as humans are able to fly in the air, then there really is no limit to what we're able to accomplish.

"Sir, the plane is ready to leave," the stewardess said.

I came back to my senses to find a stewardess in front of me, and a roaring airplane ready to go.

"Thank you very much, ma'am."

I rushed up the steps of the plane and quickly found my seat. I breathed a huge sigh of relief as the plane took off and flew into the air. I looked through the window to my right and all I saw were clouds and blue skies. *I never imagined that I would be where I am right now,* I thought. I was sitting still in my seat, but my mind was racing. I was finally doing what I had dreamed of ever since I was a kid: flying. December 3, 1965. It's a date that I know I'll never forget.

But then, it was time to focus on the task at hand. I began writing questions for the British author I would hopefully soon be meeting. As the airplane continued seamlessly flying through the sky, providing not only popped ears and transportation, but inspiration and wonder.

SOPHIA BALDWIN is a sixth grader at Hamilton International Middle School. In addition to writing poems, she also writes very compelling science fiction.

The Saga of Vor

I am Vor Jarlswife the Fearless, or at least that's what I have the crew of Sheepscry thinking. I am Vor, that's true at least, but Jarlswife? Fearless? They think I come from northern Finland, a place I've never seen. I do not even know if there is such a place as Sharkbridge, though these people here would never consider that their wonderful Vor the Fearless could really be a liar.

I still feel the sting of the nettle field against my feet and the ache in my legs from months of walking. They can't see that though.

The Norwegian king, Horic, has asked me, the pretend Jarlswife from a pretend village in Finland, to lead a voyage to explore the west. The news of my "husband" and me has spread to very far away. No one minds that we have black hair and looks so different from anyone else around here. That was taken care of when I told them that we had visited Asgard, their land of the gods, and that their King God, Odin, had given us our beautiful black hair as a gift. They ask us many questions about what we saw in their Asgard.

Now the crew was boarding the Sheepscry. I recognized most of them, but one, an old man who was missing an eye, stood amongst them. I watched carefully, as everyone else climbed aboard. The man just stood there. "Well?" I called. "We'd like to be going!"

"The worlds are collapsing, one by one. Ragnarok is coming to Midgard. It can be stopped. Hurry; time is running out." With that the strange man disappeared.

One moment he was standing there and the next he was gone. Things like this did not happen to runaways and liars. I had witnessed magic! But I couldn't let my excitement show.

"Ragnarok? Ha, go around making a fool of yourself. Nice going, Old Man. I did like his magic trick; wonder how he pulled that off." I chuckled so they knew that I didn't believe anything that had just happened.

"But that was Odin! Surely you must have respect for the man who you met in Asgard!" someone exclaimed.

"Of course, I was only kidding."

How was I supposed to know? Then I remembered: Ragnarok was the day when the worlds were supposed to collapse and then rebuild.

"Oh no, Ragnarok. I am so... scared," I said halfheartedly.

Somehow, my incredible acting skills were failing me. Acting was my natural talent; I was always proud of how I could pretend to be anything and have people believe me.

My mother would say I was becoming honest.

I never thought that I would actually be on my crew's side. I was in this with my friend, the phony jarl. But now our ships were headed toward England, and they were defending King Athelstan from the raid that we were planning. My friend, Johan, had betrayed me. We had journeyed from western Asia all the way to this strange land together, and now this.

We all attacked at once, hopping down from the ship and swinging our weapons. It was a great entrance that I had carefully instructed them to do. Yet this got us nowhere. I was captured, along with the sheep-mistress Astrid Vlatedo.

Stupid Johan was captured by the Sheepscry, which he deserved. Now I am a slave instead of a leader, which defies the entire reason I came to this odd world. I almost want to go home and give all of this up.

All of the years of planning, this long travelling to reach Denmark: all for nothing. But aboard the Serpent's Poison, a new leader has been elected. So maybe if I stay a while longer and learn how to be a good leader, then one day I can find a new ship and lead it well. Or I can just go home.

A play of iron
Took my luck
No sweat from sun was taken
It seems as if
The day has been a waste

I set my pen aside from where I was drawing useless slashes of ink against the floor of the deck. I had little memory of letters I had learned to write back at home and my attempt at the Viking poetry was not going well.

A play of iron
Took my luck

No sweat from sun was taken

I stared at the black letters drying on the wooden boards. The sweat from sun means gold.

Ottr's Ransom also means gold. *Ottr's Ransom,* I wrote on the deck. I'm not sure but I think that Ottr's Ransom has something to do with the little girl who lived far, far away in a country so different from this one, who was teased and tormented until she ran away to Denmark and was in charge of a ship, and was then taken as a slave by another ship and then...

Alright, that has nothing to do with Ottr's Ransom.

After many days of sailing, we caught sight of a beautiful island of white sand. The foolish King Horic was paying us to discover new lands. This was perfect! It was a blur of blank white waiting to be built on. We sailed closer. Suddenly, pieces of the island started to split off and drift towards our ship. They were white stags, creatures legend to eat bits of the nine worlds. There were millions of them.

They had just started to tear our ship apart when two of Astrid's sheep leapt off the ship and chased them away. The sheep rode white stags at the end of the pack. They bit and kicked until the stags were just dots on the horizon. We never saw those sheep again.

Astrid had bragged about her amazing fighter-sheep before, but I had never believed her.

"Why didn't you tell them to fight back in England?" I asked.

"You never ordered me to. You were the captain, remember?"

Ragnarok is coming!

The realization hit me as I was sitting beside the poetry on the deck. If the white stags are real, then Odin is real and Ragnarok is real.

A play of iron
Took my luck
No sweat from sun was taken
Ottr's Ransom

The words wounded random, but really they were a constant reminder of how I had been taken from my ship.

A play of iron
Took my luck

The words were embedded in the wood. Why had I written on the deck? Who would have ever thought to write on a ship's deck? Now how could I ever feel like I was part of this ship? I got my pen and quickly scrawled new words across the wood.

A play of iron
Took my luck
Though now, aboard a newer, better ship
I'm glad no sweat from sun was taken
Ottr's Ransom is what we will find

One day, as we headed towards Greenland, I was making my way towards the revised poem when I saw the one-eyed man from when I was back on the Sheepscry. He was kneeled over the poem, writing hurriedly with my pen! A moment later he sat my pen down and disappeared. Again.

I quickly read the new words, which were in my old language. How had he known? Odin was the god of Knowledge, I remembered.

There is still luck left to be taken.

Our jarl appeared behind me. "What are you looking at, Vor?" he asked.

"Letters." I almost said, "A message that Odin taught me to read during my time in Asgard," but I wasn't the jarl's wife anymore, I had nothing worth lying for.

"I am reading letters," I began. "The letters come from far away. I'm not really from Finland. I'm from Asia. I ran away to be with my friend and he pretended to be a jarl and I pretended to be his wife. I'm reading a message Odin wrote and it says that bad luck is coming.

The jarl was silent for a few seconds; this must have been very surprising news. Finally he sighed and responded, "Well, nice job, Vor. You fooled us all. And if there's bad luck, I suppose we'll have to turn around. Hopefully King Horic won't be too mad."

Our jarl didn't tell anyone, so he had to make an excuse for why we turned around. He told everyone it was because of a storm that had already caused us to lose lots of our supplies.

We sailed back to Norway, offering King Horic everything we had. He refused most of it, though he was glad that we had passed on the message Odin had given me on my first day aboard my original ship.

Johan hated the life of a Viking. He ran away. To home. I stayed in Scandanavia.

I still had to help stop Ragnarok with the crews of Sheepscry and the Serpent's Poison. Soon, the two ships are scheduled to sail around the nine worlds. And the jarl told me it was about time to for me to get a higher rake.

The Serpent's Poison has a new attempt at a poem written on it. I think I did a better job this time, though I'm not sure.

That play of iron
Was the last
No more luck
Was ever taken

The Loki girl
Is like Loki no longer
Her luck refilled
Ottr's Ransom

JESSICA DARLINGTON is a mainstay at The Greater Seattle Bureau of Fearless Ideas' After-School Tutoring program, and is in seventh grade at Salmon Bay School. She also plays volleyball.

Orchid Adventure

"Hey, everyone! I found a new species of orchid!" the new botanist yelled. "It is somewhere in the Amazon. I must go there and find it and bring it back!"

"Be quiet," yelled the other botanist. "You go back to your magic fantasy land so we can get to work." The new botanist's name was Mark Dawn and he was very smart. He was going to find that orchid, and in one day he was going to the Amazon to bring it back.

That night, Mark gathered all his information, pictures, and files about his new orchid. After packing his suitcase, Mark clicked "Buy ticket to the Amazon," on his computer. Three minutes later, he was fast asleep. The next morning, he ate breakfast, hailed a taxi, and was on his way to the airport.

After an exhausting eighteen hours on a plane, Mark was in the Amazon looking for his orchid. The first day of looking for his orchid, all he got was twenty-three mosquito bites. That night Mark camped out with a tribe that lived in the jungle. They put aloe on his bug bites, and in the morning they were all better.

Then he went even deeper into the jungle, finding orchids related to the one he was tracking. The jungle was humid and Mark was getting tired, but he kept going and found a huge tree with beautiful orchids. From where Mark was, he couldn't tell if the orchids were his. So he threw a rope over a branch and climbed up. Yes, they were Mark's orchids— bright orange with pink speckles. He pulled out one of the flowers and climbed down.

Mark was so happy to have tracked down the new species of orchid.

When he got back to the botanist lab, he showed off his orchid, which was called the Dawn Orchid. The botanists never doubted Mark again.

ZÖE NEWTON is fourteen years old and is a ninth grader at Ballard High School. In the future, she would like to live in every country and travel the world with cats. Cats should be involved.

Penguin Vacation!

Since penguins are adapted for cold climates, and some are able to live in warmer places, I would recommend to a penguin to come to Seattle. It isn't too hot or too cold at all, and there are plenty of sights to see.

I would assume that a penguin would love to see the men at the market throw fish back and forth, and finally decide to stop torturing himself and eat lunch at Ivar's. Then he could attempt to make friends with the seagulls down by the piers. Unfortunately, he may be prohibited from swimming there.

While he is exploring the docks, he could visit the Aquarium, where there are yet more fish for him to fantasize about (and, of course, learn about.) And, just like anyone else, I'm sure this particular penguin would love to see the unique Space Needle in downtown Seattle.

Then, one day, the manager at Men's Warehouse may catch him waddling down the street, compliment his exquisite taste, and offer him a job as a tuxedo salespenguin. He can move to Seattle and make tons of money to buy the fish he dreams of.

JENNIE SHORTRIDGE is the author of five novels, including her latest, *Love Water Memory*, a three-time Indie Next pick and Library Journal Editor's pick. When not working on her own books, Jennie has been known to teach writing workshops for The Greater Seattle Bureau of Fearless Ideas and other organizations. She's also the co-founder of nonprofit collective of authors called Seattle7Writers, who raise money and awareness for literacy in the Northwest.

Night Flight

ıⁱˡ·ıˡˡ|ⁱ·ı111ˡ·ıˡ·ıˡ·ıˡ|ıˡ·ı111|ⁱ|ⁱ·ıˡ|ˡıⁱ·ı111ˡ·ıⁱ·ıˡ·ıˡ|ıⁱ·ı111|ⁱ1

It was a grand and terrible thing at dusk, when the bats flew up and out of the mine shaft, all at once like the dinner bell had clanged somewhere in batville and bug-eating must commence immediately in this flurry of waxy wing beating and tittering fur. We'd sit there with everyone else from town, watching with varying degrees of curiosity and revulsion as the plume spread across the sky. Pop and Elsie and I would be drinking our Dewar's and Cokes in lawn chairs, waving off the heat of the day with our hands, trying to recall exactly when the bats had started making Laporte their summer home.

I'd never even thought twice about the bats before Pop brought Elsie home from Spokane to live with us, saying, "You know your mother would want it this way." I didn't know that at all, as my mother was still alive and married to him, though she'd been confined to the grounds of the Joyful Pines Nursing Center for nearly ten of her sixty-three years. To be fair, her mind had gone wandering earlier than most, and Pop always did have a thing for what he liked to call "classy ladies." At least Elsie was closer in age to him than his previous choices, but he'd never brought one home to live before.

"We could go watch the bats at twilight," Elsie suggested—most likely as a way for the two of us to bond, as I was still acting pissy at that point—and she packed up the cooler with fixings for drinks and what she liked to call "nibbles:" Port wine cheese and hard salami, expensive crackers, even though Pop and I'd always had a thing for Ritz and Tillamook. Elsie's tastes ran a bit richer than ours in all things, and Pop liked to say she upped our game, even though he'd never liked it when my mother spent an extra dime on anything, let alone a five-dollar box of crackers.

You didn't used to be able to even find five-dollar crackers in Laporte, but things started changing when folks gave up on the mine and turned their attention to skinny young geeks in big glasses instead. All those worker-bees who'd answered the siren song of

Mr. Gates were starting to retire, or just wanted to live in the country, and like Elsie, they brought their upwardly mobile tastes with them. Wilson's Food Mart would have been crazy not to oblige them, but once old man Wilson had his fifth and final heart attack, his kids got greedy. After that, to get decently priced milk and eggs and meat, you had to go clear to the Super Kmart eleven miles east of town.

But I have digressed from the bats. Perhaps I am more like my mother than I like to think; I am approaching the age she was when folks in town started to call her "dotty Dot," that point in her midlife when she started getting lost driving home, and did things like put on her pantyhose in the Wilson's parking lot in broad daylight right after purchasing them.

People say that's why I never married and why I stayed home with Pop, to take care of him after she couldn't anymore, but the real reason was I had no urge to leave. Like the bats with their homing instincts, only I never migrated in the first place.

I had a good job at Meisner Realty doing bookkeeping and light cleaning. There weren't that many men around who weren't married or, well, odd. And I suppose I was a little odd myself, living with my Pop my whole life, but like he said, "If it ain't broke, it ain't broke." And the last thing I wanted to be was anything that resembled broken. What Pop didn't say was that at the first sign of disrepair—say a toaster that burned too hot?—you got tossed out in the trash. Or, if you were really unlucky, sent to live in an old folks home.

So, we'd sit there at the mine with our drinks, Pop and Elsie and me, getting just past tipsy. The bats would fly up like a cannon blast of cinders from the silver shaft, filling the twilight with a pixilated haze (pixilated being a word you never used to hear until everything started changing, just like those five-dollar crackers). People would exclaim, "Oh my!" every time they took flight, even though we all came out night after summer night, July through early September. Most of us wore hats or brought umbrellas for protection from the raining guano, and even though everyone knows that bats won't really get tangled in your hair, we felt a bit more confident about it when under cover.

Except Elsie, who refused to compromise her classy lady updo, preferring instead to just wave a pink floral scarf over her head when necessary. This was especially ironic because she was the one who took it upon herself to supply us with all manner of bat factoids she'd read on the Internet, including the "humans are too large as prey" tidbit. So when that bat flew straight into the center of her beehive, I knew everything was about to go haywire.

In truth, I'd felt it coming for a long time.

The first thing was that my mother got sick, and I don't mean the Alzheimer's. The dementia did make it harder to notice the cancer, they said, because she wasn't telling anyone about throwing up blood, and she'd never eaten much. A month was all they gave her, but she couldn't even hold on that long. I read all the materials they gave me about this being a special time with your loved one and how you could connect and share and get closure with him or her, but between my mother not knowing me and being in that much pain, there wasn't a lot of connecting or sharing going on. She'd call out for me, and I couldn't convince her I was right there. It was more suffering than you allow a stray dog to go through before putting it down. She died with hot wild eyes staring up at nothing, no one there for her, just a stranger telling her she loved her, telling her to let go, for god's sake, and get it over with.

The second thing was the bats falling out of the sky, and I like to think it was in homage to my mother, whose illness was as surely caused by the mine as the other twenty or thirty people in town who'd succumbed to some form of cancer, only no official would ever say it.

Zoom, up those bats went that last night in August, the night of my mother's cremation, and everyone watched and *oohed* and *aahed* as if they were at the fireworks, until the first bat came hurtling back to earth, and then the second. At first we thought it was just a guano-heavy night, and then maybe that some kid was throwing dirt clods or their gnawed chicken bones. Pretty soon, though, we knew what it was, a rain of bats, and it didn't matter if you had an umbrella or not, you ran like hell to get away from the carnage.

The last thing was that Pop ran off the next day, just left Laporte and Elsie and me behind in the middle of the night as we slept. What he did take with him was my mother—all soft white ash and fragment in a plastic box—and I can only hope he found a suitable resting place for her remains and his sorry carcass that does not include yet another classy lady.

Elsie seemed less surprised at his departure than I was. A week or so later, she went to live with my boss, Mr. Meisner from the realty office, whose wife had left him the year before when he was caught blowing soap bubbles in his car with a Laporte High School cheerleader, whose green and white uniform lay neatly folded on the seat between them. They weren't doing anything wrong, exactly, so the story goes, but I can see that it would be difficult for a wife to imagine that could be so.

On the day Elsie moved out, she sat me down in the living room and said, "Look, I'm real sorry I shacked up with your dad, him being married and all. I thought he was over your mom, but I guess she wasn't so broken he couldn't love her anymore." That may have been the moment I realized how much I'd gotten to like old Elsie, in spite of it all. At least she said goodbye.

The bats all either died or migrated on by the end of summer. The state came in and collected a few of the dead to autopsy and discovered that it was, of course, the mine tailings that had poisoned them. They found even more dead bats lying inside the shaft; it seemed the ones who'd upped and died in flight had arisen just to throw us a warning:

We are all of us impermanent beings, but if you stay too long in toxic places, your time may come sooner than you'd like.

Come spring I asked Mr. Meisner to stick a sign in the yard. I agreed to work the open house the first weekend, seeing as Elsie wanted him to go home to Spokane with her to meet her sister. I sat in our kitchen, dressed like a realtor in a skirt and blouse, and yes, pantyhose from Wilson's, and had each person, even the neighborhood lookie-loos, sign in and take a brochure. "Great location and value priced fixer upper!" it read, Mr. Meisner's wording, even though Pop and I had always kept it neat and in good repair.

A couple who were expecting snatched it up after seeing it that first day, talking about how they were going to tear out walls and change the roofline and get rid of the horrid carpet, and how on earth could anyone live in such small spaces, in such, well... *conditions*? I might have let it slip as they were leaving that it was, in fact, my childhood home. I think that might be why they agreed to pay full price, which was, at that time, ten percent over market.

I live in Henderson now, twenty-seven miles past the Super Kmart and eons away from even the most adventurous yuppie. It reminds me of how Laporte used to be when I was a kid: a little store with a gas pump, a post office, and not much else on Main Street but weeds and a few derelict Victorians. Most of us up live up the hill in old logging cabins, with perfectly cozy small rooms. What we don't have is a mine, or Port wine cheese, or judgmental young pregnant women. And I am especially grateful not to have spotted one classy lady. Granted, there are even fewer prospects here for male companionship than there were back home, and I doubt I'll ever have a place to go and visit the nicer memories of my mother, but I can live with all that.

I can live with almost anything, now, knowing the bats around here have the good sense to roost in trees.

MARGOT KENLY is famous at The Greater Seattle Bureau of Fearless Ideas as one of our most generous supporters, which includes sharing her terrific ideas. For example, she was a major visionary for this book you are holding and helped launch us into major hotels throughout downtown Seattle. She was also the Founder and Head of the Santa Barbara Middle School. She then moved to Seattle and started The Famous Pacific Dessert Company, The Original Mariner Biscuit Company and most recently Blue Dog Bakery (natural dog treats). We are so lucky to have her as a devoted friend of The Greater Seattle Bureau of Fearless Ideas.

Loose in the Kitchen:

How a Kid-Friendly Illinois Brownie Recipe Made Pacific Desserts Famous

This wasn't the first recipe created by Pacific Desserts, but it might have been.

When I started Pacific Desserts in 1980, I made mousses and cheesecakes for about twenty-five restaurants in Seattle. I heard about Michael Mooney, second trombonist for the Seattle Symphony, who made flourless torts and tarts for two restaurants in town. I had extra space at the bakery that I originally sublet to him, but we got along extremely well, and it became clear that his desserts would be the perfect addition to Pacific Desserts. I ran the retail stores/wholesale business and Michael, no longer with the symphony, was responsible for the production.

We began to build our recipes. I told Michael that the restaurants wanted a carrot cake. We both had recipes, and decided to bring them in and taste them. I took one bite of his carrot cake and threw mine in the garbage. His was amazing, the best carrot cake I had ever eaten.

The other request was for a really good chocolate brownie. So we did the same thing, Michael brought in his brownie recipe and I brought in mine.

The recipes were identical. Ingredient for ingredient, step by step, in the exact same order, word for word, identical. I asked him where he'd gotten his recipe. Both of our recipes were written out by our mothers on funky three-by-five cards. I grew up in northern Illinois, and Michael lived in southern Illinois. We think the recipe must have been in the *Chicago Tribune* back in the 50's and both of our mothers had cut it out.

This was the first recipe I ever made by myself, when Mom let me loose in the kitchen on my own. It is a recipe a child can make. Well, it has to be made in a double boiler, so a child with a double boiler.

The brownies are designed to be dramatically undercooked. Normally, if you put a knife in a baked dessert you want it to come out clean. Not with these. Most people overcook brownies and they dry out. As long as they're really moist, the chocolate flavor explodes in your mouth. You can make them with or without pecans.

We ran Pacific Desserts for twelve years, and it has long since ended. I still see Michael, we're fast friends, and he still makes these brownies, too. Our company was more famous for our "Chocolate Decadence," but we consider the Family Brownies as our first true recipe, and they'll always be as close to my heart as the yellowed recipe card with my mother's handwriting on it.

Family Brownies

Preheat oven to 350°F. Place shelf in the middle of the oven.

In the top of a double boiler, melt:
4 oz. unsweetened baking chocolate
1/2 lb. (two sticks) unsalted butter
When fully melted, pour into mixing bowl.

Add:
2 cups sugar
1 cup flour
4 eggs, slightly beaten
generous pinch of salt
1 tablespoon vanilla
1 cup chopped pecans (optional)
Grease a 9" x 9" pan and coat it lightly with flour. Pour in batter.

Bake for 35 minutes. Center will still be soft. Place pan on a rack to cool before cutting.

Makes 16 thick brownies. (Recipe can be cut in half and baked for 18-20 minutes in 9" x 9" pan.)

Photo by David Rzegocki

53

MATTHEW SIMMONS is the author of *A Jello Horse* (Publishing Genius Press, 2009) and *Happy Rock* (Dark Coast Press, 2012). He lives in Seattle.

Americans After America

ıₗıₗıₗıₗₚ·ıₙₙₙₗₗₗₗ·ₗ·ₗ·ₗₗ·ₗ·ₗₚ·ıₙₗₗₗₗₗₗₗ·ₗₗₚ·ıₗₙₗₙₗₗₗₗₗₗₗₗₙₗₚ·ₗₗₗₗₚₙₙ

And so there came a day when, as one, the Americans arrived at a thought. It was suddenly clear and obvious and irrefutable: America—their beloved, vast, well-developed country—was, in fact, not really theirs. They had taken it—with boats, with muskets, with blankets soaked in disease, with numbers. (Oh, so many numbers.) And the full meaning of that—of them having taken their country—hit them all at once. The magnitude of it. The consequences of it. The possibility that there was really a lot of injustice in it.

And arriving together at that thought, the Americans did what Americans were so famous the world over for doing. Because the Americans were—at bottom—a just people, because the Americans were—at heart—a good people, and because the Americans were—in a pinch—a generous people, the Americans decided that, after all the years of American history (which they had acquired in first a handful and then a large pile of states united together for the purpose of acquiring a history) that it was time they maybe went ahead and left those states to the original owners, to let them take it back over, to let them maybe come up with a new government, to let them maybe come up with a new flag, to let them decide if they wanted to, say, keep the border configurations as is, or perhaps come up with a whole new setup or whatever.

Because, really, whatever. It was going to be their country again. The Americans thought it gauche to make suggestions on their way out. (Because the Americans were, we all know, a humble people, uninterested in meddling in the affairs of others.)

It was, as I said, quite sudden. There they were, these Americans, watching televised football or watching televised poker or checking the Internet to see about their fantasy football teams or playing online poker, and then they had their epiphany. "We should maybe go," they said to one another. They had that tone where what they said was both a statement and a question. Like, they asked a question but ended it in a period.

"Should we maybe go."

And yes, they all agreed. They should probably go. And they should probably not make a big deal out of it, too, because Americans were—you might remember or you might have been told—not into making a big thing out of things. They like to be subtle. They didn't care for drama. Americans were inconspicuous.

The Americans packed up travel bags. A small few packed heavy. Most packed light. Americans traveled in so many different ways. The Americans left behind most of what they had acquired over the years and years they had spent living in America—a place wherein the acquisition of things was made easy in a way that was the envy of the rest of the world, but was also sometimes seemed to the non-Americans to be tacky. But, in fact, the truth about the Americans and their will to acquire was more complicated than it seems when only the surface of the American character is analyzed. Unpack the American zest for the gathering of and subsequent use of or storing of things, and one finds that hidden within it, buried in the recesses of the American psyche were the seeds of the American expatriation. Always there within was the *leaving*. Implicit in its founding, the Americans looked toward their great sovereign state's dissolution—like every birth announcement carries in it, subtextually, the coming obituary. The Americans implanted in their character an acquisitiveness not because they lacked tact, but because they desired to leave a lot of things behind for the original owners of the land they had called America to offer some recompense. And that is exactly what they did. They left almost all of it behind. In their houses. At their offices. In the safety deposit boxes. In hidden safes with combination locks. The Americans left it all. And on kitchen tables, they left notes. Notes that said:

"Hey, sorry about all this. You can keep the stuff, if you want. Because, I mean, our bad and all that."

Spiritually speaking, the Americans were made stronger by the sudden loss of so much acquired consumable material. Or, the sudden casting off of said. Walking away from all the things weighing them down—please forgive the cliché—made a much lighter people of them.

So, small bags packed, a map or two, a guidebook, and with all the American airlines and ocean liner owners and rail services agreeing to make final gratis runs out of the country to far-flung destinations, the Americans, in the dead of night, left. So the story goes, they sang as they set out for the world. So the story goes, the National Anthem was neglected because a consensus could not be reached on all the lyrics—a second verse? A third? A fourth? Did anyone really know them?—and no American could adequately deal with the vocal range needed to properly sing a song that, we don't hesitate to point out, had been chosen specifically for the ambition of its melody. (Because the Americans were an ambitious people.)

Not a one could hit the notes. Not a single American. And because the Americans were a realistic people, they did not try. They choose, instead, the song that both spoke to the American character and that fit the American pitch limits. So the story goes, they sang "Take Me Out to the Ballgame."

Here's what the Americans learned when they left America and entered the world as Americans after America, as the American diaspora:

—Americans learned new languages. Attached as they had been for so many years to the English language, the one they had borrowed from, well, the English, the Americans learned that they needed to—in certain places, anyway—become familiar in rudimentary or comprehensive ways with new languages—the languages of the world. (The ones, they were happy to admit, that had so flummoxed them when they were still in America.) So they did what they needed. In their own inimitable American style, the Americans went online and bought audio files of recorded language instruction. For long months, the Americans walked the streets of their new homes—in Europe, in Asia, in Africa, in Australia—earbuds inserted deep in their ears, sheepish, apologetic looks on their faces when they accidentally stepped out into traffic or bumped into a stranger and were unable to apologize in the local language, and the Americans learned. As Americans liked to do. They walked around with their iPods or other mp3 playing devices held in their hands and they listened and they mumbled to themselves with just a little self-consciousness. "Petit dejeuner," they said. "Watashi wa John Smith desu," they said. It should be noted, though, that no matter how hard they tried, the first Americans after America never truly lost their accent, no matter what language they used to replace English.

And over time, English itself began to loose its global ubiquity. The language that had become the language of international business—because of American corporate power—was allowed to isolate itself once again to the obscurity of the British Isles and the Australian continent. And in its place, Chinese took over as the dominant language of international conference calls and meant-to-impress client dinners.

—The Americans learned the great pleasure of being outside. At first, the Americans approached their new surroundings like tourists. They had so many new places to discover, so many old buildings to stare at and, in groups, to comment on the ages of to one another. (America, for all its history, was such a young country. Its buildings were all so new. To be around so many old buildings was, in the words of many an American, "Totally GD charming. Can you believe how charming it all is? Look how old!") So, the Americans approached their new homes in touristy sorts of ways, in touristy sorts of outfits, with touristy kinds of attention. Before the Americans found themselves settling into whatever lives they were going to make for themselves in their new homes, the Americans sight-saw. And with all this time outside, walking around, the Americans began to find that they enjoyed the sun. They enjoyed the physical activity. They enjoyed getting a little tan below the sleeves of their shirts, and they enjoyed wearing visors. They enjoyed cafes, and they enjoyed decks overlooking the streets, and they enjoyed the random attention of cats and dogs that had made the streets their homes. They enjoyed strolling.

The Americans, after learning a great affection for being in the out-of-doors, eventually found work in the out-of-doors. Many had left office jobs in America, had left cubicles and desks and hands-free headsets for multi-lined phones, but in the world, the Americans gravitated to work that involved the use of their hands, and a ceiling not of square, replaceable panels, but of sky. Light not from buzzing fluorescent bulbs, but from the big, yellow sun.

—The Americans learned to eat butter. The Americans learned to ride public transport to and from work. The Americans learned how to have affairs, and be aware of friends having affairs, without telling anyone about it, to cultivate tact and avoid gossip. The Americans learned to take longer vacations. The Americans learned to write letters to one another, actual letters that they put in envelopes and mailed to the friends they'd had back when they were Americans in America. The Americans learned to read books, and to find a way to allow themselves the free time to read books. The Americans learned how to listen to the stories older people told, and learned to remember them, and learned to take lessons that they could apply to their lives from them. The Americans learned to cry when they were happy. The Americans learned to laugh off rotten luck. The Americans learned—truly, truly learned—how to spot and really appreciate irony.

The world did not immediately accept the Americans. They were Americans after all. They had a reputation. Not a bad reputation, necessarily. Not a good reputation, either. They simply had a reputation. They had a reputation for being Americans. And the world remembered what they had been like when they were Americans with an America. Some remembered it when the Americans had invaded them, and it was not a happy memory. Some remembered a time when they had hoped the Americans would invade them, and it was also not a happy memory. Some remembered aid to dictators. Some remembered the lack of aid after a natural disaster. Some simply remembered that time when the American basketball player dunked on one of their own during the Olympics, and the way he had grabbed his crotch, and let out a loud howl, and they remembered not really thinking that behavior was very sporting.

These new Americans—these Americans without an America—remembered those things, too. Not always in the same ways, sure. But they remembered them. And they made a humble face. And they held up their hands. And they said, "Sorry about that. But, hey, here we are. Mind if we move in next door? We keep our lawns neat and we love to invite neighbors over for barbecues and such."

They did not blend in, the Americans. And they tried to blend in. They really did. But they never really could. First generation. Second generation. Third generation. They spoke their new languages as Americans—with their flat, American accents. They wore their new clothes as Americans, with a tightness at the collar and a looseness at the waist. They ate as Americans, drank as Americans. Made friends as Americans. Worked as Americans. There was some essential nature to them, some aura around them, something—perhaps just a particular way they walked—that continued for a long time to mark them as Americans. And this, for a time, made the world uncomfortable. Just a little.

But, really, it didn't bother the Americans. They did not feel as if they needed to be ashamed of their American-ness. They enjoyed it. And because the Americans had an enthusiasm about themselves as Americans, eventually that enthusiasm infected the people of their new homes. It infected the world.

The world learned from the Americans. More than anything else, the world learned a happy kind of urgency. As the Americans learned to slow down, the world learned to speed up, and somewhere in this came a kind of cohesion. As the world ingested the American character, and as the Americans allowed themselves to be consumed by the world community, the American-ness became a kind of nutrient. This American-ness flowed in a great planetary bloodstream and it fed and it fed and it fed the world. So, for a time, the world had this rhythm to it. This pulse. This charge. It was exciting, the world moving ahead, maybe not paying as much attention to its heading and its destination. Just moving, and moving so fast that half the history that was happening didn't even get written down. Because who had time to write anything down? Because everything just wants to move.

Eventually the Americans—without their America, within the world—melted away. Became history. Assimilated fully. Generations passed and the accent mostly disappeared, and the clothes began to fit right. And the once-Americans became not Americans without America, but Russians in Russia. And Australians in Australia. And Indians in India. And Germans in Germany. And some even became French.

But a bit of the charge is still here. The world still pulses a little from the infusion of Americans it got all those years ago. And sometimes you'll meet a person, and you'll talk to that person, and you'll get to know that person, and get to like that person, and you'll notice within that person a quality. And you notice it but you don't say anything. And they notice you noticing it, and they don't say anything, either. Because Americans never liked to make a big deal out of things.

This Really Happened:
Family Tales

To really get to know someone, write their story. The eighth graders of Jessie Towbin and Joshua Medaris' classes at Big Picture Middle School in Burien did just this, writing creative non-fiction biographies about someone in their family. Students brainstormed a list of biographical questions, interviewed an older relative, then crafted their notes into narrative non-fiction pieces that told the story of a significant time in that person's life. Their stories were compiled in a chapbook they named *This Really Happened*, and read to volunteers and parents at an end-of-project celebration.

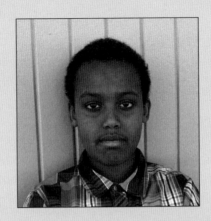

ABDULAHI ABDI is fourteen and is a student at Big Picture Middle School. He chose to write about his father, Abdiqani, because he was interested in his childhood in Somalia. When it rains, he likes to play video games. One day, he will go to Somalia to see his grandmother.

Abdiqani's Life

Somalia—what a hot place. It is over ninety degrees there every day and it is home to many deadly creatures like the black mamba, a really deadly and poisonous snake; the lion, a fierce predator; and the hyena, a thief and a coward. If you go to the savannah in Somalia, it is very likely that a lion will chase you. One day that happened to Abdiqani, an active, strong boy who had a lot of energy. He was playing in the savannah one afternoon when he heard a roar. He quickly turned around and ten feet away, staring at him, was the biggest lion he had ever seen.

Abdiqani always saw lions, but not one like this. Its teeth were huge—the size of your index finger—and drool dripped out of its gaping wide mouth. Its long, thick mane made it look tough. Its claws were sharp enough to cut through a ten-foot wall of titanium. Abdiqani thought, *it's over.* Then he ran. The lion roared and chased after him. Abdiqani was running like crazy, zigzagging everywhere. His heart was beating with the speed of a cheetah. He had no weapons to protect himself.

Then he saw a big tree and he climbed it. The lion curled up under the tree's shadow, waiting patiently. After several minutes the lion noticed a gazelle grazing in the field nearby. It stayed low while creeping toward the gazelle. Suddenly the gazelle noticed the lion and ran. The lion chased after it.

As soon as the lion ran away, Abdiqani climbed down the tree, ran back to his village and told his friend what had happened.

His friend laughed and said, "Wow, Abdiqani, you have a wild mind!"

Abdiqani said, "It is true, I did get chased by a lion, the biggest one I have ever seen."

His friend said, "Yeah, whatever, keep lying. Oh, and don't forget we have to go to visit our relatives in the city on the other side of the savannah in a few days."

So the next week, Abdiqani and his friend left the city in the morning and they walked for a while. It was a day's walk. They had been before, but it was their first time going alone. The savannah was really big. Soon the clouds had an orange glow as the sun was about to set. They realized they were lost.

Abdiqani said, "We should camp out. I'm really tired."

His friend replied, "No we should keep going, then camp when we find out where the city is."

So they kept on walking. Eventually they were under a clear dark sky. Then they finally laid down their blankets. Just as they were about to fall asleep, the sound of evil laughter from behind them woke them up. They turned and saw what looked like four dogs staring at them. They heard the evil laughter again.

"What is that?" Abdiqani's friend said.

"Dogs don't laugh. Hyenas do." said Abdiqani.

"I'll hold them off, you run!" said his friend. He began throwing rocks while Abdiqani ran. Abdiqani picked up rocks on the way, and when his friend was out, he threw rocks while his friend ran. It went on like that for ten minutes until a man camping nearby heard the commotion and came with a gun. He shot and killed one of the hyenas. The others hyenas got smart and ran away.

The man asked, "What are you kids doing here in the middle of the night?"

"We were going to the city but the hyenas came and tried to attack us before we went to sleep," his friend replied.

The man asked, "Need a lift to the city? I am going there right now."

They said yes so the man gave them a lift in his jeep. He took them to Abdiqani's relatives' hut in the city. His relatives were surprised to see him in the middle of the night. They were shocked to hear what had happened, and happy the boys were safe.

This all happened to my dad before he came to the United States. This story shows that Abdiqani was a brave young man who cared about his friends and family, and he still does.

JENNAKA TATON is fifteen. Jeanette is Jennaka's mother. Her
grandmother, Jane, passed away the same year Jennaka was born, so she
never got to meet her, but she's heard lots of stories—the good and the
bad. Jeanette and Jennaka have a great relationship that can also never be
broken. One day, Jennaka will be a professional dancer.

Coco's Car House

When Jeanette moved in with her mom, there was a huge problem. Her mom, Jane, did not have a big, fancy home or an apartment. Jane lived out of her 1969 Chevy Bel Air. So that meant Jeanette had to live in the car with her mom. Jeanette was the oldest of three kids. Her parents had divorced when she was nine years old. She only lived with her dad for three months, then she decided to leave to live with her mom.

At first, Jeanette was super-scared to live out of a car. But things at home with her dad were much worse. So she packed up a brown paper bag with her little clothes and one toy, a small stuffed panda bear named Coco.

Every morning, Jeanette would brush her teeth in a sink at a gas station, and have a snack from the nearest 7-Eleven. Then Jane would drop her off at school. Only then would Jeanette see her brother and sister. They would cry and cry because they missed Jeanette at home and they were kind of jealous that she lived with their mom. But they had no idea it was out of a car.

As time went on, Jane and Jeanette would stop at different friends' homes to eat or shower. Then at night, they would sleep at a local church parking lot.

Jeanette said these were really tough days, but really happy days, too. It gave Jeanette a chance to really get to know her mom. There were a lot of times they would laugh and pretend they were undercover FBI agents or world travelers. Sometimes they would be scared, and it would be over a cat jumping on the car. They would just laugh and laugh because they were chicken FBI agents. Jeanette never missed a day of school and always finished all of her homework. Jeanette said it was nice to finally be the only kid for a while.

Jeanette's dad never knew she lived out of a car with her mom. In fact, not one family member had a clue, except for the few friends that knew.

One day, Jane dropped Jeanette off at school and went to work. While she was at work, someone broke into the car and stole Jeanette's only toy, Coco. Jane was so upset when she saw what had happened, and she could not even imagine how Jeanette would feel. She was filled with sympathy for her daughter.

That day after school, Jeanette jumped in the car and knew something was wrong. Jeanette could not breathe.

"Mom, something's wrong," she said.

"I know. Someone broke into our car," Jane said.

"How did they get in? The windows don't look broken," Jeanette said, processing the news.

"No broken windows, but they did take some money. And Jeanette—they also took Coco," she said, putting a gentle hand on her leg.

Jeanette cried and cried for days. This may have been nothing for some kids, but it did affect Jeanette's childhood. She became very guarded over her things and hardly shared.

Jeanette learned many lessons from this story—never leave your prized personal things unguarded; learn to share, even if you really do not want to.

Jeanette says do not be sad about this story, because even though she lived almost one year in that car, it was the most awesome year. Being with her mother and really getting to know her helped them both become a tighter family, and they knew that bond could never be broken. It has helped Jeanette relate to others when hard times come up.

Epilogue

The most memorable part of this story happens màny years later. Jeanette went to college and had to do a timeline of a small part of her life. In this timeline was this very same story. Jeanette received an A on that report and was approached by a publishing company to write about it. Jeanette was truly flattered, but declined the offer. She explained that sometimes it's best to keep some stories to yourself. Except for now.

DAVID B. WILLIAMS is a freelance writer focused on the intersection of people and the natural world. His books include *Stories in Stone: Travels Through Urban Geology* and *The Seattle Street-Smart Naturalist: Field Notes from the City,* in which this essay appeared. He has recently finished his next book, *Too High and Too Steep: Reshaping Seattle's Topography*, which will be published in 2015 by the University of Washington Press. He maintains the blog GeologyWriter.com.

The Stone

I found Rome a city of bricks and left it a city of marble.
— Augustus Caesar

The character, the sources, and, above all, the behavior in use and durability of the building stones in a large city should be matters of interest to architects and builders, to students of economic geology, and to the general public.
— W. O. Crosby and G. F. Loughlin, *TecÙology Quarterly*, 1904

I majored in geology in college for two simple reasons: physics and field trips. It wasn't that I liked physics; it was my complete ineptitude—I once got a sixteen percent on a three-hour quiz—that forced me to abandon my original plans of getting an engineering degree and designing bicycles and other forms of human-powered vehicles. With the engineering option eliminated, I turned to the course I had enjoyed the most.

In the *Introduction to Geology* class I took my freshman year at Colorado College, we had taken a week-long field trip through Colorado, Texas, and New Mexico. We had visited hot springs, examined 1.8-billion-year old fossils, crawled through caves, and whacked rocks in some of the most beautiful scenery I had ever seen. I still have two rocks I collected on that field trip. Over the next three years, I took another ten geology courses, the highlights of which were the one week per month we spent on field trips to places such as Grand Canyon, Rocky Mountain, and Arches national parks.

During those four years, I found that what I liked most about geology, in addition to the field trips, was learning stories about the planet's past. I liked knowing about ancient rivers and volcanoes, long-dried up seas, and plants and animals that once lived. Each of these stories helped connect me to the places where I hiked and lived.

After graduation, I moved to Moab, Utah, to work and teach in one of the Nirvanas for rock hounds. For nearly a decade the red rock canyons, arches, mesas, and cliffs permeated my life on a daily basis. I became addicted to seeing, learning about, and traipsing over rock, particularly sandstone. When I moved back to Seattle in 1998, I went into rock withdrawal and had to seek out the closest examples I could find—the building stones of the downtown area.

I began to wander the business district gawking at buildings. I saw granites from Minnesota, Brazil, China, and India, fossils from Germany, France, and Indiana, and rocks that formed between 80,000 and 3.5 billion years ago. I found that several buildings incorporated stones from quarries first used by the Romans over 2,000 years ago and that a controversy in the construction of the downtown Metro bus tunnels forced King County officials to return $500,000 in "tainted stone." In learning to read the stories of building stone, I also developed a new appreciation for the intersection between people and geology.

Like many cities, Seattle can trace its use of building stone to fire. On June 6, 1889, John E. Back, described in the *Seattle Post-Intelligencer* as "a thick-set blond of mediocre intelligence," let his pot of glue boil over and onto the stove in Victor Clairmont's basement-level cabinet store near Front (now First) and Madison. Back acted eagerly but incorrectly, and tossed water on the flames, which merely spread the fire to wood shavings on the floor. Soon the entire wooden structure was burning.

Flames spread like a bad rumor across the business district. Like most young towns, especially those in the West, early Seattle had built its downtown out of wood, the most abundant local material. Before Seattle's "Great Fire" could be contained, it burned over 115 acres and destroyed the downtown retail and industrial core. The Great Fire clearly showed one of wood's weaknesses, particularly in a town without adequate water pressure to put out a blaze. Within days the upstart, proud town vowed it would rebuild, but this time it would turn to a local material that could better withstand fire—rock.

Builders started with local sandstones and granites, but soon sought out rock from Vermont and Indiana for variety. As additional money and people flowed into Seattle over the subsequent decades, owners desired more exotic material and found it in rocks from Italy and Sardinia. Finally, as cutting techniques improved and transportation became cheaper, the worldwide stone trade began to resemble plate tectonics, with granites and marbles traveling across the planet, propelled by the demands of builders.

When I need a rock fix, I often go downtown to Pioneer Square, because it contains so much sandstone, some of which I can even walk across. From foundations to support walls, grayish-green sandstone also dominates the many buildings, such as the Pioneer, Grand Central, and Terry-Denny, which popped up within a year or two of the fire. Most contain two-foot-thick blocks of rock—thick enough to support a multi-story structure and to withstand fire—known to geologists and builders as Chuckanut Sandstone.

On one of my periodic expeditions to explore downtown Seattle's geology, I stop by the Pioneer Building, a striking edifice with an arched entryway topped by two rows of what look like stacked sandstone donuts. On the south side, I find several window sills where I can peel up an individual, 1/8-inch-thick layer of sandstone. This spalling occurs because water penetrating the layers of sandstone has deposited salt crystals, which have slowly grown and wedged apart the sandstone strata. Further damage occurs during the infrequent Seattle winters when the temperature drops below freezing and ice forms. When water freezes it expands about nine percent and has the same damaging effect as salt crystals.

Only a handful of the Chuckanut blocks have layers weakened enough for me to pull off. Building technique plays a role in weathering rates. If a builder stacks sandstone blocks with their beds vertical and parallel to the building's surface, like an upright book face out on a shelf, then the agents of erosion can weaken the stone so that beds peel off one layer at a time. If the beds lay horizontally, like a book flat on a shelf, water does not easily penetrate the layers and the rock deteriorates more slowly. Ledges, such as the window sill I had found, are the most common place for building stones to weaken because they are not protected by other rocks. Stacked blocks generally resist weathering better but salt and ice can also degrade them.

Examining my recently detached chunk of Chuckanut with my 15x magnifying glass, or hand-lens, I see specks of black, clear, and white minerals—hornblende, quartz, and feldspar, respectively. I rub the chunk between my fingers and minerals break off and leave gritty grains in my hand. If I close my eyes, I can pretend I hold sands from my beloved red rocks of Utah.

The Chuckanut was one of a triumvirate of sandstones that started to appear in downtown buildings in the 1890s.[1] Bellingham quarries supplied the Chuckanut, while other quarry sites near Tenino, 12 miles southeast of Olympia, and Wilkeson, 15 miles east of Tacoma, provided rocks known by their locality name. These quarries, which opened as early as the 1850s, succeeded because they combined proximity to water or rail transport with a homogenous, well-cemented, low porosity rock.

Despite the 125 miles separating the quarries, they share a related geologic history. The great beds of western Washington sandstone were deposited 40 to 50 million years ago when this region was warmer and wetter. Judging from the fossils found within the Chuckanut, geologists have evidence that palm trees, swamp cypresses, and tree-sized ferns grew in the moist, Louisiana bayou-like environment.

The area that would become western Washington lacked the dramatic topography that now dominates. Neither the Cascade Mountains nor the Olympic Mountains existed. Instead, a broad, low-elevation coastal plain extended eastward into central Washington.

Waves from an ocean that spread to the west washed ashore on beach front property, or what we now call the I-5 corridor. What mountains did exist rose far to the east along the Washington/Idaho border. Rivers and streams washed out of those mountains and meandered toward a coastal lowland dotted with seasonal lakes, swamps, and lagoons. As the rivers spread toward the ocean, they deposited bed upon bed of sand, eventually building up a many thousand foot-thick layer cake of sandstone. Most of the sand grains accumulated where water slowed down at the inside edge of bends in rivers.

These beds or strata are what give sandstones their typical appearance, which many have likened to a layer cake. The layer-cake pattern and subsequent salt- and ice-induced splitting of layers is the main reason why sandstone is no longer a popular building material. Builders still use sandstone but if you see sandstone blocks they are more than likely on an older building and more than likely a locally derived rock. [2]

Sandstone was not the only western Washington rock to become popular after June 1889. Builders also turned to a salt-and-pepper stone, known as Index granite, quarried 35 miles northeast of Seattle in the hamlet of Index. John Soderberg, a Swedish immigrant and founder of Swedish Hospital, opened the quarry in 1893, after the Great Northern Railroad laid tracks along the Skykomish River. Rock from this quarry soon began to appear in the city as structural foundations, paving stones, curbs, and quoins.

The Smith Tower, built in 1914, is Seattle's best known building with Index granite walls, although they only make up the first few stories. A two block walk south and east from the Pioneer Building brings me to this splendid skyscraper, once the ninth tallest building in the United States and tallest west of the Mississippi for many decades.[3] Compared with some other granites found in Seattle, the Index granite is more heterogeneous and less flashy. Furthermore, the variously sized blobs of black and white in the Index do not appeal to those who want consistency in their building stone.

Geologists, on the other hand, like these blobs, or enclaves as they call them, because of the insight they provide into the formation of granite and other closely related rocks. (Quarry workers called them 'heathens' due to their unwelcome presence spoiling the uniform texture of the rock.) For example, white enclaves indicate a gas or water pocket in the magma, or molten rock, that cooled to form the Index. The black ones are pockets of iron- and manganese-rich molten material that moved up through the Index magma, like the movement of colored blobs in a lava lamp. You may also find bits of sandstone that fell off the chamber walls in which the magma crystallized, but they are rarer.

The Index granite formed 34 million years ago, after a wedge of oceanic crust, the Juan de Fuca plate, pushed eastward by tectonic action, bumped into the North American continent. The cold, iron- and manganese-rich oceanic crust then began to dive under the lighter continental material. As the Juan de Fuca slid deeper, it descended into the

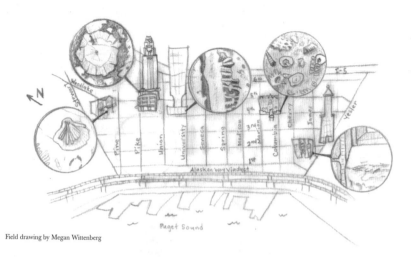

Field drawing by Megan Wittenberg

asthenosphere, the 40- to 120-mile-deep layer of hot, partially molten rock that transports the dozen or so plates that comprise the outer layer of the planet. As with a stick of butter thrust into hot water, the leading edge of the Juan de Fuca began to melt, creating molten rock or magma, which started to rise.

The magma crept higher and eventually pierced the bottom of the North America plate, where it began to cool and crystallize into the Index granite. In some places, the magma continued to rise through the plate and burst onto the surface, forming volcanoes. A pulse of Juan de Fuca subduction, which may have started as recently as two million years ago and continues to the present, is also responsible for the state's five modern volcanoes.

Igneous rocks, such as granite and basalt, are the superstars of the rock world. In addition to starring roles in bad, geologically questionable movies (*Volcano* and *Dante's Peak*) or headlines (Mt. St. Helens and Mt. Pinatubo), igneous rocks also play a significant part in using stone in building in this country.

When architect Solomon Willard walked over 300 miles in 1825 to find the perfect granite for the Bunker Hill Monument, it led to the construction of the first commercial railroad in America. Because the quarries were too far from water, engineer Gridley Bryant proposed a 2 3/4-mile long railroad from the rock to the Neponset River. Horse-drawn cars, with 6 1/2-foot tall wheels, carried the loads, which averaged six tons each. More recently, some critics also argue that when Philip Johnson and John Burgee used Connecticut granite on their AT&T Building in Manhattan, they started a revival in stone-covered buildings. Granite dominates the modern building trade because it is hard, colorful, and weather resistant.

From the Smith Tower, I walk east and north over to the Rainier Club at Fourth and Columbia to examine one of the earlier non-local rocks to appear in Seattle. The club, built in 1904, is mostly brick but also contains white to buff limestone blocks quarried near Bedford, Indiana. The rock is known as the Salem Limestone and is one of the most commonly used building stones in the United States.

In Seattle, one can find Salem blocks at the new Seattle Art Museum (the old is made from Wilkeson Sandstone), the Seattle Branch of the Federal Reserve Bank of San Francisco, and the *Seattle Times* building. Other widely known Salem buildings include the Empire State Building, Grand Central Station, the Holocaust Memorial Museum in Washington D.C., and San Francisco City Hall. As far as I have been able to discover, the Salem is the only building stone used in all fifty states.

Deposition of the building stone section of the Salem Limestone occurred 300 to 330 million years ago in a quiet, tropical sea that spread across an area that would become the Midwest. At that time most of the land mass now known as North America lay south of the equator. As in the Bahamas, where future limestone is forming, the sea was clear and shallow. The warm waters supported a diverse range of swimming, crawling, and bottom-dwelling invertebrates. When they died, their bodies collected in a watery cemetery on the sea floor, eventually solidifying into a 40- to 100-foot-thick stone menagerie.

Getting out my trusty hand-lens, I examine the limestone blocks that cap a long wall of brick on Fourth. At 15x magnification, the Salem becomes as intricate as a Pointillist painting except that tiny corpses have replaced the dots of paint. Most of the fossils that I find are the shattered remains of shells destroyed by long stilled tidal action. I distinguish many fragments of pelecypods or bivalves, the animal class that includes oysters, clams, and scallops.

Crinoid stems, 1/16 to 1/2-inch-wide discs, are the most common recognizable fossil. They come from animals, closely related to starfish, sand dollars, and sea urchins, that lived at the bottom of the sea. Crinoids resemble a wildflower with a root-like base attached to the substrate, a stem of varying length and consisting of discs stacked like poker chips, and a flower- or fan-like top. Now much less common than their ancestors, modern crinoids tend to live in inaccessible parts of the sea.

Another common fossil fragment resembles Rice Chex cereal. This was the housing complex of a microscopic, sedentary animal known as a bryozoan. The fan-shaped, Salem bryozoans lived in colonies of interconnected rooms. Water flowing across the net-like structure provided food for the hundreds or thousands of organisms that formed the colony. Other fossils include brachiopods (clam-like shellfish), gastropods (snails), and ostracods (minute crustaceans that also resemble clams).

After carefully probing this long extinct ecosystem, I head north to a building that typifies the modern use of building stone. Unlike Seattle's earliest structures, which used massive blocks of stone for structural support, the City Centre building (5th and Union) is clad in one- to two-inch thick sheets of rock that hang like skin on a steel infrastructure. This practice of using stone merely for decoration is one reason that so many different varieties of rock from so many different continents now can be used as building stone. It is why I am so happy to explore downtown buildings. City Centre, for example, uses rocks from Africa, Sardinia, and Finland.

My favorite of the three is the red Finnish granite, quarried about 30 miles southwest of Helsinki. It crystallized approximately 1.6 billion years ago and is known by geologists as a rapakivi granite, and by builders as Porkkala Red. [4] I like rapakivi granites because of the ease of distinguishing them from other rocks and because of their unusual age and distribution. Once you find one in an urban environment, it is quite easy to impress your friends by tossing out a few fun facts.

For instance, I start out by saying: "Few other rocks display the unusual texture of a rapakivi. Most have one- to three-inch long, ovoid, feldspar crystals, either red or pinkish, often rimmed by greenish-gray, plagioclase feldspar. The Porkkala lacks the rimming but does display first rate microcline, a potassium rich feldspar. Another good example is the 1000 Second Avenue building, which uses a rapakivi called Baltic Brown."

(Geologists have argued for decades about how this texture formed, with no side producing decisive, unequivocal evidence. They do agree, however, that the large feldspar crystals indicate slow cooling underground. As a group, feldspars are the most common mineral of the Earth's crust. They occur in all three of the broad rock types, igneous, metamorphic, and sedimentary, and range in color from white to sky blue.)

Once I have dazzled my friends with a textural analysis, I add a few notes on the unusual age of rapakivi granites. "The majority formed between 1 and 1.75 billion years ago with an average age of 1.54 billion years. No other type of granite magmatism fits in such a tight time frame. So when you see one on a building, you can feel confident that you are most likely looking at rocks that crystallized several hundred million years before the first recognizable forms of life existed." [5]

And finally, I electrify them by addressing rapakivi distribution. "Although they occur on all the continents, rapakivis are generally restricted to the oldest, most stable part of these landmasses, called by geologists the continental craton, or shield. Geologists value these rocks because they are important evidence for how the continents formed and aid in the understanding of plate tectonics."

When confronted with such fine information, most people get a glazed look in their eyes of what I perceive to be pure contentment and happiness.

Leaving the exciting world of rapakivi granites, I retreat south a block to the Rainier Tower and its cavity-filled, oatmeal-colored base of travertine, one of the few building stones in Seattle you can interact with. Travertine is a type of limestone that lacks fossils and does not form in the sea. Instead, it precipitates from calcite-rich water associated with springs or caves. Mammoth Hot Springs in Yellowstone National Park is a good modern example. As water spilling out of a spring evaporates, any solids carried in solution settle to the ground, like the settling of spices in Italian salad dressing. In travertine, calcite is the primary solid, building up layer upon layer, as long as the spring continues to expel water. The holes found in travertine indicate deposition around plants. Millimeter-wide, yellowish calcite crystals fill many of the spaces.

While no one is looking, I take out a bottle filled with Modenaceti Balsamic Vinegar and splash some of the dark liquid on the calcite crystals. They immediately start to fizz when the acid in the vinegar reacts with the calcite, producing carbon dioxide and water. Passing the fizz test is one of the key indicators of a limestone. Most geologists use dilute hydrochloric acid or even distilled white vinegar for the test, but we in urban environments have to make do with what is at hand.

The Rainier Tower panels are the youngest rock in Seattle—around 80,000 years old. They were quarried near Rome in the town of Tivoli, where people have built structures out of the easy-to-cut rock for over 2,000 years. Well known travertine buildings in Rome include St. Peters, the Quirinal Palace, and the Colosseum.[6]

Just north on Fifth from the Rainier Tower rises the Washington Federal Savings building, also built with travertine, but a structure that saddens my geologic heart. Overzealous builders filled each hole in the building's travertine with some sort of cement or goo. My guess is that the builders were not concerned with renegade geologists wielding salad dressing ingredients but thought that the rock required a bit of preventative maintenance. In a colder location, such as Boston, water seeps into the cracks, freezes, expands, and weakens the rock. Seattle's moderate winter climate, however, has little effect on the creamy rock. About the only problem here comes from urban pollution that discolors the travertine.

This oatmeal, black, and green building also displays Seattle's most controversial type of building stone, a rock known in the construction trade as Verde Fontaine. South African quarries produced this pine green rock, which solidified underground over one billion years ago. The green coloration comes from the mineral chlorite, which forms from the alteration of iron- and magnesium-rich minerals within the rock.

The conflagration over Verde Fontaine began in early January 1989. During the construction of the city's underground bus stations, Eddie Rye of the Black Contractors

Coalition notified the tunnel builders, Metro, about the planned use of Verde Fontaine in two of the downtown stations. This directly conflicted with a resolution that Metro, which manages King County's bus system and collects, treats, and discharges Seattle's sewage, had passed only 16 months earlier that prohibited the use of materials "fabricated or manufactured" in South Africa, because of apartheid.

After Rye blew the whistle, Metro Executive Director Alan Gibbs said that even though the use of the rock technically was not illegal because it was only quarried in South Africa and cut and finished in Italy, using the South African granite would "taint the project forever;" therefore, Metro would drop the Verde Fontaine from the project, costing hundreds of thousands of dollars. Citizens and public officials both praised and castigated Gibbs' decision to stop using the green granite. After six additional weeks of meetings, debates, and public input, Gibbs resigned. The tunnels opened on September 15, 1990, with walls covered in less polemical rock.

I am not surprised that contractors may not have known of Verde Fontaine's South African origin. Jerry Williams, an architect with the tunnel's design firm, TRA, said at the time that designers choose a building stone to go with the color scheme and normally don't know where the stone is quarried. I found this to be the case when I was researching this story. Many architects and building managers that I talked to proudly said, "We used Italian granite and Italian marble for interior and exterior walls," no matter where the rock originated.

I don't think they purposely meant to mislead me; they were just misinformed. Many of the building stones used in Seattle were cut and finished in Italy, regardless of whether they were quarried in Finland, Australia, or South Africa. Contractors often send rocks to Italy because of lower cutting costs and a higher quality end product. Therefore, buyers only know the Italian connection and no more.

Shipping to Italy also has an additional benefit. One geologist told me about a white Australian marble, which, when transported to Italy, acquired a new name, Carrara Marble—best known as the marble made famous by Michelangelo—because Italians cut the rock. Which would you rather buy: Michelangelo's marble or some Outback rock?

Abandoning controversy and degraded travertine, I continue north on Fifth Avenue to my final destination, the Westlake Center, one of the dullest architectural locations in Seattle. This is one of the best parts of urban geology: even ugly buildings might contain intriguing geology, giving me a reason to examine them. I have disliked this building ever since the Westlake office tower and shopping mall were built, replacing the big hole left by the removal of Bartell's Drugs. The City missed a splendid opportunity by not creating a small downtown green space, but I console myself with the geology.

Upon entering Westlake Center, I get down on my hands and knees. Two people ask me if I have lost a contact lens—Seattle is such a friendly place. I shake my head and return to my perusal of one of the best fossil exhibits in Seattle. The floor of Westlake Center is made from blocks of a red streaked, tawny limestone quarried about 15 miles south of Dijon, France, which geologists call the Comblanchien Limestone. The fine-grained mud that solidified into the Comblanchien settled in shallow, lagoon-like waters protected by sandbars. The water was an arm of a sea that covered Europe roughly 175 million years ago, during the Jurassic age when dinosaurs gallivanted across the planet.[7]

Bottom-dwelling organisms dominate the Westlake fossils. This includes sponges, small mounds of filter feeding organisms, that fossilized into dark blobby shapes that stand out from the surrounding ecru matrix, and solitary corals, which from the top resemble a clock face without the numbers and from the side look like an ice cream cone. Brachio-pods, marine animals often mistaken for clams, were common in one slab, while another block contained a few snails.

The fine-grained quality and pureness (99-100 percent calcite) of the Comblanchien have made it a popular building stone since the Middle Ages. Like many stones used in the building trade, the Comblanchien's fame spread with the railroad, which reached the quarries during the reign of Napoleon III (1852-1870). The limestone has remained pop-ular in France and is found in Orly Airport, the stairs of Sacre Couer and the Musee d'Art Moderne, both in Paris.

Jurassic-age French limestones play another role for some Seattleites. Grapes that make many of the finest burgundy wines, such as Beaune, Nuits St. George, and Cham-bertin, grow on soils derived from these rocks.

When I asked the architectural firm that designed Westlake about this rock, no one mentioned the fossils. Instead, I was told: "I believe we had that rock specially made for us." I have asked other people in the building stone trade the age of a particular rock and had answers ranging from "a few thousand" to "as old as the hills" to "several billion." The last answer is my favorite even though it is often the most imprecise. At least the person who made this ambitious claim realizes the great age of Earth and might even believe in evolution.

Lack of geological literacy is symptomatic of our general absence of understanding of the natural world around us and yet ecological and geological processes affect us every day. For example, when I teach geology programs for school kids at the Burke Museum of Natural History and Culture, I like to ask if any students deal with rocks and minerals on a daily basis. Most say "No!" I think that many adults would offer the same answer; yet these students watch their teachers write with chalk, which is made of microscopic fossils; put a mineral known as salt on their French fries; take Tums, which are mostly calcite; and attend school in a building often made of rock or brick.

Because geology (and all aspects of the natural world) play such pivotal roles in our lives, I think it would be nifty if great works of natural history (or even basic texts) shared space with great works of literature on everyone's personal bookshelves. People could take pride in being able to accurately describe a rapakivi granite, state the age of Earth, or converse intelligently about evolution. I know that not everyone has had formal training in the sciences but if they need a place to begin their reading, I can recommend a good building or two.

Endnotes

1 The best source of information about building stone in the state is Dave Knoblach's *Washington's Stone Industry—A History* (Washington Geology: v. 21, no. 4, pg. 3-17) Perhaps the best known stone structure is the capitol building in Olympia. Built between 1922-1928, the dome is one of two self-supporting stone domes in the United States.

2 Weathering by salt and ice is a fate met by many sandstones in urban environments. Probably the best known sufferers are the ubiquitous brownstones of New York and Boston, which were popular from the mid 1800s to early 1900s. These eastern rocks are essentially the same as our local variety, starting life as sediments washing out of a now eroded mountain chain, 200 million years ago when dinosaurs frolicked across a tropical New England.

3 The Smith Tower opened on July 4, 1914 after four years of construction. Lyman Cornelius Smith was a former shotgun manufacturer turned typewriter maker (Smith Corona) when he decided to build his tower in Seattle. He died before completion of the building. The only taller buildings were in New York City. Smith Tower remained the tallest building west of the Mississippi River until construction of the Humble building in Houston, Texas, in 1963.

4 Rapakivi is a Finnish word meaning "weathered rock" or "crumbly stone" from *kivi* = rock or stone and *rapautua* = weather (verb). The term originated because the Finnish rapakivis tend to disintegrate more easily than other granitic rocks of the region, not necessarily a good endorsement for a building stone. Granite comes from the Italian *garnito*, meaning grained.

5 Rapakivis are not the oldest rocks used in Seattle's buildings. That crown goes to the Morton Gneiss, a 3.5 billion year old rock, quarried in Minnesota, and found in the Seattle Exchange Building.

6 The word travertine comes from the Italian *travertino*, a corruption of *tiburtino* or the stone of Tibur (now known as Tivoli). In the fifteenth and sixteenth centuries, builders pilfered travertine from the Colosseum and used it in the Piazza di San Marco in Venice and Pallazzo Farnese in Rome.

7 A fossil-rich layer of German limestone deposited at this time makes up the floors of the entry and elevator floors at the Grand Hyatt Hotel in downtown Seattle. The slices of gray rock contain some of Seattle's largest building-stone fossils, up to four-inch-wide ammonites, which look like a top view of a cinnamon roll. Ammonites were relatives of squids and octopuses. They went extinct at the same time as the dinosaurs, 65 million years ago.

Into the World:
Stories Abroad

Before starting to write their fictional stories set in exotic locales, the fourth grade students of Angie Armburst's class at Viewland Elementary School researched a country of their choosing for a social studies and geography unit on world cultures. Many of the students' stories were set in the country of their own heritage, including Russia, Morocco, Panama, and Ethiopia. The students then took the details from their reports and incorporated them into original fictional tales set in their chosen countries. The students titled the chapbook of their stories *Into the World: A Place You've Never Been Before.*

DEANGELOS CLARK is a fifth grader at Viewlands Elementary School. He was inspired to write a story set in Panama because his relatives used to live there. He aspires to be a scientist or a football player.

The Nightmare

In Panama, even though it is beautiful, it does not mean that people are beautiful. For example, Manuel Noriega was a bad dictator. Would you want to be his friend? I didn't think so. But, guess what? He is the person we are going to hear about today, so get comfortable and get ready for awesomeness.

Manuel came into power in 1983. He kept weapons from when he was in the Panama Army. If the people of Panama were the superheroes in this story, then Noriega would be the villain. This is why people can make bad comments about him: because he did bad things. He hit the Panamanian people and sometimes killed them. Manuel was not always mean. He was bullied like crazy when he was a kid, so that is why he became evil.

At night, he would practice his evil laugh.

"Har har har!" he would say. He sounded kind of like a pirate.

Because he was a dictator, he got whatever he wanted or else something bad would happen. He wore his army outfit every day to scare people and remind them he was a general. He started a lot of wars with other countries and after every war he would eat bananas to celebrate his victory.

"No one better touch my bananas, or else!" he would say.

One day, after a long war between Panama and Havana (a city in Cuba), he was craving a big dinner.

"Hurry up! I want sausage, eggs, rice, and bananas, now! And I mean a *big* dinner!" Manuel said in his evil, mean, yelling voice.

His servants hurried to serve him. Manuel was so disrespectful that he burped at his servant and said, "Shooooo!" so his servants ran like lightning back into the kitchen.

Each time Manuel ate a meal he wore a special navy shirt that was green, black, and kind of plaid. He smacked his food until it was all gone and left his plate and silverware on his golden table for his servants to clean while he went upstairs to his bed.

"That was a good dinner, but my servants were lousy," he said.

He got his favorite Dalmatian puppy pajamas on, and practiced his evil laugh until he fell asleep. He snored until the moon went down and the sun rose and things got started again.

After a long sleep he got dressed in his khaki pants with his army uniform and got ready to go to the Panama Canal to check if everything was okay and that the oil was being shipped.

"Some of that oil should be for my hair!" he laughed.

That morning, he was running late because he had thrown his alarm across the room at a servant the night before, and so he'd slept through his strict scheduled wakeup time. He was so late, he had to skip his usual sausage and egg breakfast. Usually, he got around by people carrying him on a fancy bed, but he decided his servants were too lazy and slow, so he stormed off and decided to run by himself the few miles to the canal. When he got there, what he saw was his worst nightmare—it was a nightmare he could not wake up from. At the canal, there were hundreds of Panamanian navy guards waiting for him. He was confused. *Did I tell them to go there?* he thought.

One of the guards got a hand on him.

"What is going on? Let go of me!" Manuel yelled.

"We don't like you anymore! You are not a good person to serve! All of Panama is turning against you!" the guard said. Manuel had done mean things to the guard's family, so even though it was risky to stand up to him, the guard was just done with it. He decided to make his own orders, and turn against Manuel.

"Really? ALL of Panama?" said Manuel. "I'll execute the entire country!"

"That won't happen because you'll be in jail probably for the rest of your life!" the guard said.

"Hope you like cells!" said another. They arrested Manuel and put him in jail.

After four months, Manuel went to trial in the courtroom. No one showed up to root for him. Even his lawyer didn't want to be there. He avoided eye contact with Manuel, and stood as far away from him in the courtroom as he could.

The judge took a really deep breath before sentencing him. "You are removed from power and will spend thirty-three years in a Panamanian jail for assault and battery," he said. Manuel had his head down in disappointment. His lawyer smiled. The people of Panama had a huge two-day parade to celebrate him going to jail. Even the judge took off his robe and went to join in.

In Manuel's jail, there was really tight security. There were guards everywhere, so if he tried to escape he'd be caught. He didn't even have a bed to sleep on. Instead of wearing his army uniform every day, the guards made him wear his Dalmatian pajamas.

Manuel thought, *Man I regret doing all those stupid things... And leaving my servants at home!* And with that he was left in his cell, crocheting.

"Rats!" he said.

HELEN SERESTE is a fifth grader at Viewlands Elementary School. Three of her goals are to be better at tetherball, practice improving her voice, and send money to her family in Ethiopia. When she grows up, she would like to be a singer or a doctor.

First Sight At Last

Lena got ready for the party in her town, Addis Ababa. She put on hair curlers and her purple dress with short ruffled sleeves. The dress was traditional. Her test to become a brain surgeon was in fifteen days and she had to study. She was driving to the party but she was worried sick about the test.

Fifteen minutes later she was at the party and on top of the roof. There were blue streamers. The lights were off, but there were disco balls, four in the corner and one in the middle of the party.

How fun, only girls and NO BOYS! thought Lena. Well, there was one boy, her friend Elsa's brother, Harold, whose nickname was Harry.

Lena fell in love at first sight. And OMG there was too much food and she tasted some really good injera.

"How much did this injera cost?" she asked her friend Elsa.

"We made it at home," said Elsa.

"I can't believe the weather, it is so hot out," Lena told her friend.

"It is like 100 degrees out," said Elsa. "Of course, we are in the middle of the equator," she added.

"I love that the food is spicy with a touch of sweetness," Lena said. "Injera is my favorite!"

Just then, Elsa saw Lena staring at Harold.

"If you like him, make a move," said Elsa.

"Really? That wouldn't feel weird or awkward?" said Lena.

"No, not at all," said Elsa.

"Thanks," Lena said, and she made a move.

Lena walked across the room and bumped into Harry, who was talking to his friend, Dustin. Harry turned around, "Hey, what's your name?" he said.

"My name's Lena. What's your name?"

"Harry," he replied.

"Sorry for bumping into you," said Lena.

"It's okay," said Harry.

"Are you mad?" said Lena.

"No, how could I be mad? The world famous Ethiopian King is coming to our party!"

"Abate Berhe?"

"No, that's his servant!"

"Oh, yeah. Alemnesh Tekle, then?"

"No! That's the Queen!"

"Oh, right! Haile Selassie!"

"Yes!" replied Harry.

"My dad knew him!"

Twenty minutes later, the king had come and gone and the party was over. Fifteen days later the test was over and Lena passed! She became a brain surgeon and married Harry. They moved away from Addis Ababa because they only had a thousand dollars, which wasn't enough to live on in a city where even injera was a hundred dollars. They were going to miss their family and the Ethiopian lakes and rivers, but Lena and Harry had always dreamed of moving to a peaceful place like Costa Rica.

So they moved there, and they had a very peaceful life.

JESSICA MOONEY is a Made fellow for fiction at Hugo House in Seattle and also works in the field of global health. Her writing has appeared in *Salon, The Rumpus, City Arts Magazine, RIVET Magazine, Prevention Science,* and *the Journal of Health Disparities Research and Practice.* She is currently working on her first novel.

The Mythology of Aubrey Lee

I killed my hillbilly father off with cancer—twice. The first time I was in kindergarten. During snack time, my teacher asked the class what we did for Father's Day. Casey Owens described baking fancy cupcakes with butterflies on top for her dad. To upstage her, I blurted out that mine had died of cancer. Most of the kids didn't know what cancer meant but had a vague notion it was the adult version of the boogeyman. After that, no one touched the graham crackers and juice. It was my first lesson in how to be a buzzkill.

The second time I gave my father cancer, I was on a plane to Chicago. The woman next to me had just lost her mother and was flying home for the funeral. She was about my age, mid-20s, and in and out of tears while traveling solo in the middle seat. When the man on the other side of her ordered a scotch and OJ, she clutched at my sleeve on the armrest. *You've gotta be kidding me*, she said, looking genuinely terrified. *That was my mother's drink!* She looked more feral and alone than anyone I'd ever seen, so I told her I'd lost a parent, too, which seemed to bring her some relief. *My father died of cancer.*

The truth is I never knew my father, except that he was a redneck from Alabama named Aubrey Lee. I don't know much about his family either. Whenever I try to picture what they look like, I see a bunch of caricatures: grubby-faced rubes hunting possum or whittling wood—recreational sports of the hillbilly Olympics. My father packed his bags and vanished into thin air when I was under a year old, leaving behind a space only mythology could fill. I heard he tried to kidnap me as a baby, stealing me from my crib and sneaking out through the sliding glass patio door. After I screamed and soiled myself for twenty-four hours, he handed me back over. That's the thing about kidnapping infants; their neediness and lack of self-control make them incredible hostage negotiators.

I learned about death and disappearing from the soap operas my grandmother watched as she browned onions in the kitchen. It was a creative education in exotic maladies and suspicious endings. I studied resurrection, too. The first time I saw a character on "Days of Our Lives" return from the dead after being blown to smithereens by a woman possessed by the devil, I knew there was a lot of material I could use here. I had an arch-nemesis poison my father. I gave him an incurable blood disease. He also faked his own death for insurance money, got kidnapped by a gorilla after his plane crashed on a tropical island, and was held hostage in the sewers of Paris — all before I turned eight.

The legacy of my father's whereabouts changed as I grew up and changed. He was everywhere and nowhere, both alive and dead. It was clear that asking questions about who he was or where he might be was unwelcome. My father's disappearance was a classic magician's trick: saw the lady in half. Though I don't know which half I'm supposed to be looking for, my head or my legs.

One summer, when I was nine, I went with my grandmother to visit her sisters in Iowa. She and my great aunts were sitting around playing canasta and burning through jugs of Ernest and Julio Gallo pink chablis. Sometimes when the men are gone and cards are on the table, old Catholic ladies turn spooky. The sisters started prognosticating like oracles about the disappearance of the Great Aubrey Lee as I hovered in the background looking at everyone's hands. Words like "addiction," "prison," and "death" swirled around the mosquito-heavy air. Maybe my father wasn't just a deadbeat, but rather he was pulled under by something darker than his leaving. My grandmother, slurring over her sixth glass of wine, summed up her prophecy in a single sentence: "Your father smoked too much marijuana, and it killed him."

As a child, I used to dream of writing Oprah to ask her to find my father. Unable to resist my heartfelt letter, she would hire a team of investigators to track him down. I imagined our reunion. We'd meet at a diner in the Deep South, coffee spoons cradling the distance between us, thick-ankled waitresses applauding next to a revolving bakery case, camera crews weeping into the condiments. And this sparkle, this dramatic flourish, would be the anti-venom for all those years of living in a poisoned well. All those gut-shot Father's Days where his absence was anything but cinematic.

Every once in a while I try to find him. I Google his name, comb through public records. I've discovered his extensive rap sheet, mostly for possession and theft, spanning a handful of states since the early 1980s. No malevolent gorillas, no cancer. Just lists of defunct phone numbers and addresses drifting through cyberspace, all leading to discon-nected places. I often feel closest to him after I've had too much to drink. I sometimes go through the numbers, Russian roulette-style, and drunk-dial the void. I have no script, just shaky hands and numbness. Each time, there is the monotone drone of the operator. *The number you have dialed has been disconnected. The person you have dialed cannot be reached.* The last time I called the void, a young child answered and I hung up immediately. I sat for several minutes, floating in a dull, viscous paradox, everything aching with both too much significance and no meaning at all.

The first time I see a therapist, she tells me to write his eulogy. Start with what you know, she says. I look up all the synonyms for "hillbilly." *Rube, redneck, yokel.* There are a bunch of charming terms, like *hayseed*, but I wonder about their ability to stand up to the lachrymose, slightly psychedelic tone of a eulogy for the unknown undead. If you want to be politically correct, the ACLU says you should use *backwoodsman* or *backwoodswoman.* And then there's my favorite gem: *hoi polloi*, which calls to mind a bunch of country cousins dressed in Dior. Hick chic.

I write the words on Post-it notes and stick them to the refrigerator, to my steering wheel. I wait for something to speak to me but nothing does. I begin to think his eulogy is silence. The heaviness of things unsaid trying to dry on the laundry line of time, stretching from the home where I was born to an infinite unknown. Sometimes I imagine I'm standing in a field of wild prairie grass, watching my father, the not-so-dearly departed. He sits on a crumbling front porch, coaxing rye out of a bottle, a hound's jowls draped over his boots.

I've only seen two photographs of Aubrey Lee: One is a sepia-toned shot of him holding me as a baby in 1979; the other is a mug shot from June 2013, from a local newspaper in Cullman County, Alabama. My friend sent me a link to the article via text: *Is this your father?* It was an article about a massive drug bust, and Aubrey Lee's photo was at the top. Aquafresh green prison stripes, bald dome, scraggly ZZ Top beard. My friend sent another message: *I don't see the resemblance to you …*

I have only one story about my father. My mom told me that one night he flew into a rage, grabbed a frying pan and shattered her fish tank. She insists they were tropical fish she had individually named, just to punctuate her sense of loss. I imagine brilliantly hued fish with name tags floundering in the blue glow of late-night television.

My mom, who was pregnant with me at the time, raced to gather the fish with newspaper and deposit the diaspora in a bathtub of running water. Ten minutes into the rescue mission, she realized she forgot to plug the drain. She stared helplessly as the smaller fish disappeared; the larger ones jumped under the gushing faucet, their bodies smashing into shards of glass. Defeated, my mom walked back to the living room and waited for the mass piscine grave to stop thumping around her, her bare, cut up feet dripping blood into the shag carpeting. Sometimes I think my mom's still there—with me in her belly, slowly bleeding into the ground.

As I grew up, the frying pan still hung in our kitchen, next to the crocheted potholders and Mrs. Dash. Though it was little used, it lingered, collecting a thick coating of grease. Every once in a while I would take it down and feel its weight. I would invent stories about my father as I gripped the wooden handle. Mythology born from a God with Teflon skin. I would imagine the half of me I didn't know, feel for its outline and shape. I have his hair, his height. I have his yen for excess and leaving, which I keep muzzled and chained like an animal of unknown temperament. I have his name and his hillbilly bones. Aubrey Lee, a man made up of smoke and dust. A diseased limb on a defiled tree. A fish murderer responsible for the genocide of a small artery of Atlantis.

Instead of his eulogy, I wrote a eulogy for the missing. Not only for those gone, but for those never here. For the undead ghosts roaming the halls of addiction. For lives that are lost but still living. I dedicated it to all who don't know where half of who they are comes from. I spoke of how I feel tickled to pay the electric bill, eat vegetables, smile kindly at a stranger. How I marvel at these tiny, mundane acts of normalcy, and feel proud, like I haven't given in to his missing. I buried the eulogy with his photograph and raised a glass. To Aubrey Lee. To all of us with unknown blood, a family of half families. May we find our pound of flesh among the flowers.

How We See It: Personal Narrative

Proyecto Saber ("Project Knowledge") is a civic and academic support class at Ballard High School centered on Latino culture. Proyecto Saber students crafted personal narratives, working side by side with volunteers as well as prominent Northwest authors Kathleen Alcalá and Domingo Martinez, and photographer Victoria VanBruinisse. The finished products were multimedia digital storytelling pieces that combined memoir writing, photography, and audio versions of the students' stories. The work was published in a chapbook the students named *How We See It*, posted on the digital storytelling website cowbird.com, and used as inspiration for the personal statement writing portion of their college entrance applications.

ERIC LUNA RIVERA is a senior at Ballard High School. He plays all the positions on the Ballard soccer team. In the future, he wants to move to the Bay Area and be a police officer, or something like it.

The Call

｜·｜·｜｜·｜｜｜··ｍｍｌ·ｌ·ｌ·ｌｑ·ｌｑ·ｌｌ·ｌｌｐ·ｌｌＭＭＭ｜ｑ·ｌ·ｌｌ·ｌｌｐ·ｌｍｍｌ·ｌｊ·ｌｑ·ｌｊｉｐ·ｌＭＭＭ｜ｌ

I was pumped. I knew it would be a perfect night. Something wasn't right, though. I was nervous—more nervous than any other weekend night. I was feeling a bad vibe, a vibe I had never felt before.

I was shaking, more nervous than ever. It was twelve-thirtyish and I had barely left my parents' room. They were fully awake and I was aware of that, but that wasn't going to stop me from sneaking out that night. My friend kept calling, telling me to hurry up— that they had been waiting outside my house for a while and that it was cold and the girls we were kicking it with had already snuck out and were just waiting for us.

I had to make the move already. I had to get out. I had the spare keys to my mom's truck. I went out the back door and ran through my neighbor's yard. My friend was waiting for me. I made him get into the truck. I was super scared to turn on the truck because it would make a big noise and I was paranoid that my parents would hear it. I turned the truck on and pulled out of the driveway right away. We were going to Queen Anne. I was feeling weird—as if something was going to happen.

All of a sudden, I felt my phone vibrate. My heart was racing super fast, making me feel as if I had cheetahs running all around. I checked, and it was Mom. I didn't know what to do. I knew my life was going to be hell when I got home. I turned back to go home. There was no way we were going to meet up with the girls. I was caught. I was very angry and scared and kept hitting the steering wheel. I remember looking down and my friend yelling that I had almost crashed into a taxi. My mom kept calling. Then it was my dad, my cousin and even my uncle. Never did I answer.

My plan was to play like I had just gone to McDonalds. I was scared to death of facing my dad. I got a McDoubles french fries to make it seem convincing, I went crazy on the road just to get home. I was going eighty miles an hour plus up 15th Street. At the intersection by the Safeway, close to my house, I saw my dad out looking for me. I thought I was taking the secret way home, but he saw me too.

When I got home, my mom and uncle were really disappointed.

"You better go to sleep before your dad walks in," Mom said.

But I didn't. I sat down and tried eating my McDonalds but I couldn't even eat it, I was so nervous. My stomach was hurting. I was afraid. When my dad came home, it was as if the devil had walked in. He went straight for me and I knew I was going to get a beating, but my uncle stepped in and pushed him away. My dad started yelling at me and saying a bunch of stuff nonstop for, like, thirty minutes. I just went to my room and tried falling asleep. We went about a month without talking.

I learned a lot from this mistake of mine—always answer your parents' phone calls. It's a worry thing. If they can't get ahold of you, they worry more, making them imagine all kinds of bad trouble. I knew it was a bad idea to be taking the truck, because at any moment I could have crashed and died or killed someone, or have been pulled over and gotten into deep trouble. So I was glad, after all, that I had gotten caught and that I had learned my lesson. But as I always say, STRICT PARENTS CREATE SNEAKY KIDS.

FRANCES BAKER is a senior at Ballard High School. She loves music and photography. In the future, she wants to start her own foundation. She is inspired by live music and concerts, where you can never be sad.

Obstacles of Life

What gives you harmony? That soothing feeling that spreads throughout your body, that soaks into your pores and melts into your bones, that jolts into your soul and veins. Everybody in life has a purpose, no matter what—something that gives one true happiness. Well my happiness and purpose is singing.

Every day my highlight is when I go to choir. It makes me feel relaxed. It makes me feel carefree and lucky that I have an environment where I can practice my pieces with the people around me and see progress. I'm a first alto. It's a middle part so it requires a lot of listening around me. I have to make sure my harmony is good and the clashes that occur in the pieces don't sound too flat or too sharp. Ms. Pelavin, the director, points out the problems and flaws to fix for the group, but I should be able to point them out myself to improve my skills. When I'm singing, I feel like I'm actually good at something—that I can do something.

Being part of a group makes me feel responsible, but contained. Sometimes I feel like I should be heard as an individual voice, not just the one that's connected to everyone else. It makes me think about my future—how much I'll have to individually grow, not just in a group. I still have insecurities and doubts that I struggle with almost every day. My confidence and belief in myself isn't what it should be. To be happy, I'll need more independence and self-confidence.

I always have feelings about myself that make me feel like "I can't." These thoughts can control and take over my mind, but that doesn't mean I need to give in to them. I can't let these thoughts swarm me for life. When the negative thoughts start to brew in my head, singing makes me forget.

GERARDO CERVANTES-NARANJO is a junior at Ballard High School. He loves playing the guitar, skateboarding, and the ocean. One day, he would like to go scuba diving at a beautiful coral reef.

Family Music

The first time I heard music was when I was five years old. I was in an outdoor covered area by the house where my dad worked. It was a hot California night. It was even hotter because I was dancing and running around with all my relatives. I was with my whole family, all together.

My relatives were playing traditional Mexican music together in a band with a guitar, drums, and *bajosestos*—twelve-string guitars you play by hitting two strings at a time. My uncle and my grandma were the main singers. Some of the music was *allegre*—happy, upbeat. Other songs were sad and told stories of Mexican villagers falling into trouble.

I looked at all the instruments and thought to myself, *how could music come out of such strange objects?*

The first instrument I tried to learn myself was a clarinet when I was twelve in middle school band class. I hated it. Especially the way the vibration felt on my teeth.

The first time I really felt interested in playing music was a year later when I picked up the guitar. My dad taught me to play the flamenco song "La Malagueña." It took me a week trying hard to learn the individual notes. I wrote them down on a piece of paper so I could remember. My fingers hurt on my left hand because I had to push down really hard to make the notes. My right hand looked like a spider running as I played. With my thumb, I hit the guitar to make a bass sound.

When I played the song it made me feel Spanish.

After that, I started playing music all the time. I played with my uncle Cesario and my eighteen-year-old cousin, Alan. They played everything—guitar, accordion, mandolin, *tololoche* (like a bass with fat strings that you pluck). I played guitar. We didn't have a band name, but we would play together every day in the garage of the house we shared. My grandma said we couldn't play inside because it was too noisy. We played mostly traditional Mexican folk music—*rancheros* and *corridos*—and we made our own songs too.

Since then, I have gotten good at playing a bunch of instruments, including the ukulele, cello, mandolin, bass, and piano, and I even went back to the clarinet. I just moved to Seattle a year ago, and most of my family is still in Mendocino County in California, so right now I play mostly by myself in my house. I play everything from church music to metal. One day I would like to become a professional musician in a band.

When I play music I feel alive and like time is stopping around me and only music is playing.

KYLE MARSTON lives in Seattle and attended Ballard High School.

Free

ılıｰlıｰll\|ｰıımılｰlｰlｰllｍｰllll\|llｰlｰlｰllｍｍllｰlｰlｰll\|ｍlll\|ıl

When you're going down Yesler thirty miles per hour in the rain, everything else fades away.

You're not thinking about the horrified driver behind you as you bomb the red light. You're not thinking about whatever items are nestled in your bag. You're not thinking about the customer you're delivering to. It's just you, the bike, and the road. You're not ignoring the traffic: it's just a repeat. You know what the cars are going to do before they do it. The center lane is the safest because in any other, someone will open a door on you. Even if they did, there's a fifty percent chance you'll pull through. You reach the destination, lock the bike, and make your delivery.

It's the time away from your bike that gets you. You see what could've happened, but didn't. You feel how much water is in your shoes. You worry about making enough money to pay rent. But it all fades away again when you see your bike and get your next run.

When you ride fixed, the bike becomes an extension of your body. When you pedal, the bike goes. When you stop, so does the bike. Every single movement is echoed by the bike. Forget you're riding fixed and stop pedaling? You go over the handlebars. Stuck at a stoplight or track stand? Your feet become the pedals after hundreds of thousands of crank revolutions. Your foot retention is your brakes. Without them, there's nothing to stop you. When you work at a bike shop as well, it's your saving grace. When your bike has a problem, you have a problem. You're crippled by it. You need it fixed. You buy whatever you need to get it fixed. Your coworkers laugh at you for spending so much time and money on a fixed gear, but when you spend forty-plus hours a week on your bike, you're not spending money on it, you're spending it on yourself.

You fix the problem and wait impatiently for the workday to end so you can ride again. Get back to the road, the cars, and the pedestrians.

You moved out of your parents' house on your eighteenth birthday. You're thankful for all they did for you, but it's time to chart your own path in life. You work two jobs to pay the rent. You go to two schools to graduate. You shop out of the manager's special section to save money. You're tired and hungry, but you're happy. You have all you need. You have a bike, food, and shelter. Everyone says that you could be so much more. You could have it all: an office job, a car, a house, a happy family. You could be successful. But to you, that's not success. All you see are student loans, car payments, and a mortgage. You don't want these things.

You don't want something that's torn apart thousands of families. You don't want a credit score, good or bad. You live simply because you want to. Not because your financial status dictates it. You could get a blue-collar job at Boeing and watch your children grow up contentedly—grateful to you for buying the new Apple or Android gadgets. You could be everyone's version of success.

But you don't want that. You want to be your own person. You don't want to be a prisoner of someone else's dreams; you want to be free. You are free.

Megan Kelso completed her B.A. at The Evergreen State College in Olympia, where she studied history and political science, following a brief stint at art school. Inspired by the explosion of 'zines, bands and DIY art projects in the early 1990's, she self published the "Girlhero" mini comic which ran for six issues, made possible with funding from the Xeric Foundation. The comic was compiled into the book *Queen of the Black Black* (Highwater Books). Kelso received two Ignatz awards for her graphic novel *Artichoke Tales*. In 2007, she was invited by *The New York Times Magazine* to serialize her "Watergate Sue" comic as part of their weekly Funny Pages feature. Kelso is currently at work on her third collection of short stories and was invited to join the roster for the Humanities Washington Speakers Bureau's 2015-2016 season.

Kodachrome

ı¡ıˡıⁱˡˡıˡⁱⁱⁱⁱⁱⁱˡˡⁱˡⁱˡˡⁱⁱˡⁱˡˡⁱˡˡⁱⁱⁱⁱⁱⁱⁱⁱˡˡⁱⁱˡˡⁱˡˡⁱⁱⁱⁱˡˡⁱⁱˡ

Poetry and Writing of the Everyday

Creative inspiration is all around us if we just take the time to look. In composing these poems and short journal entries, students drew ideas for their writing from their explorations of the Greenwood neighborhood, and the Greenwood Space Travel Supply Company, the store that is part of our writing center.

ARCADIA SEIELSTAD is in ninth grade and is homeschooled. Already, she is a very accomplished artist and uses both drawing and poetry to inspire her creative work. In the future, she hopes to one day see the Aurora Borealis.

Sinking Peacefully

I dipped my hands into the scene of stars
The night sky rippled to my touch
I grasped the dark but it slipped away
I no longer felt troubled
I let the cold wrap around me
As I plunged into the deep dark
I thought with the liquid inspiration surrounding my body
There was no more up nor was there down
The stars were more beautiful as I got closer
I had the ideas of gods
As I lay still
Suspended in the sky
I had poetry slipping off of my tongue
I had art dancing off my fingers
It was wonderful and horrifying all at once
When I realized I was sinking
The sky was eating me
I thrashed and spun in the web
I realized
That sleeping eternally among the stars was my fate
I let them swallow me whole
And I was happy again as
I let myself drown in the light of the moon

GIN RONCO is a first grader at the North Seattle French School. She enjoys rock climbing, writing, and hanging out. She would like to travel to New York and see the Statue of Liberty.

Elephants

꧀꧀꧀꧀꧀꧀꧀꧀꧀꧀꧀꧀꧀꧀꧀꧀꧀꧀꧀꧀꧀꧀꧀꧀

Elephants are grumpy
Love lilies
Elephants fly all over the world
Pull the earth out of outer space
Hats wear elephants
An elephant is tiny
No elephant ever came to Earth
Trees are silly
So elephants are always going to be on Mars

MAX TRAN is in fifth grade and is homeschooled. He wants to be a chicken farmer, and has written about everything from board games to history in his impressive career at The Greater Seattle Bureau of Fearless Ideas.

Mountains of Poetry

CHICKENS
Eggs lightly falling to the
ground, clucking pecking
all around rooster
crowing time to
wake eggs for breakfast
until you're full but
please stay for another
mouthful

IT'S FALL/LEAVES
Leaves turning red and yellow
Falling falling all day long decomposers
Munching crunching all day long
Getting colder really colder all day long

The leaves from a tree fell
As soft as a snowflake
The leaves from a tree are
As colorful as salmon
Getting their spawning colors.

ALYSON CHEW is a second grader at Adams Elementary who likes reading and playing the piano. Her favorite animals are foxes, snow leopards, cats, dogs, and tigers. She would like to be a doctor or veterinarian when she grows up.

Yellow

ᵖˡᵖˡᵖˡˡᵖᵣₘₘₗᵖˡᵖˡᵖˡˡᵖᵣˡˡˡˡᵖˡᵖˡᵖˡˡᵖᵣₘₘₗᵖˡᵖˡᵖˡˡᵖᵣˡˡˡˡᵖˡ

Yellow sounds like happy classical music
Yellow smells like cold lemonade
Yellow looks like sun on the beach
Yellow feels like smooth sand
Yellow tastes like sour lemon.

LILLY GREY RUDGE is an eighth grader at Hamilton International Middle School. She enjoys playing the violin and writing dark and humorous fiction.

Story Makeover

Prompt: *Retell a common story (fairy tale, fable, children's story, etc.), only this time add a monster. (The monster can be evil or good.)*

Once upon a time in a gruesome land lived a monster and her name was Cinderella. Cinderella was very ugly while her stepsisters were pretty monsters. All the monsters in the land wanted to be as ugly as Cinderella. One day Cinderella got an invitation to a ball, but she was forbidden to go!

Cinderella cried and cried but suddenly a scary Godmother appeared. "Do not cry little monster," she growled.

"I will make you a disguise so you can go to the ball! Bring me a big, ugly pumpkin!" the scary Godmother ordered. When she got it she turned it into the most ugly carriage in the whole world! Then she gave Cinderella the most smelly, icky, and dreadful overalls ever!

"I love it!" Cinderella exclaimed. Suddenly three pretty white horses trotted up. "Perfect!" The scary Godmother said and she turned them into three giant ugly toads! Cinderella hopped in the carriage and rode off.

"And remember you only have until midnight!" the scary Godmother roared. When she got there, the prince started flirting with her; she punched him and left. A year later she became a professional boxer.

SADIE DOKKEN is in the second grade at Highland Terrace School. She likes going to the movies and going swimming with her friends at the lake. She loves science and would like to learn about gravity and the planets.

Wind

ꜞꞎꞎꞎꞎꞎꞎꞎꞎꞎꞎꞎꞎꞎꞎꞎꞎꞎꞎꞎꞎꞎꞎꞎꞎꞎꞎꞎꞎꞎꞎꞎꞎ

The wind in my ears
Soft leaves fuzzing in gardens
The world in my hands.

MILES RAPPAPORT is ten years old and in the fifth grade at the APP at Lincoln program. He is a big fan of obscure video games and Archie comic books.

Gutter Stars

Prompt: The famous Irish writer Oscar Wilde once wrote in one of his plays: "We are all in the gutter, but some of us are looking at the stars." What do you think this means?

I think it means, "We are all in the same mass, but some are looking at what could happen to the Earth, to your family, to you!" Things like having man reach different galaxies, or small things like growing up.

SILAS RONCO is a second grader in the APP at Lincoln program. He loves reading and hopes to be like his parents because they are his role models.

I Love It

ıₚ¹ᵤₚ¹¹¹ₚᵤₘₘₗₚ¹ₚ¹ₚ¹ₚ¹¹ₚₚ¹¹¹¹¹ₚ¹ₚ¹ₚ¹ₚ¹¹ₚᵤₘₘ¹ₚ¹ₚ¹ₚ¹ₚ¹¹ₚₚ¹¹¹¹¹ᵤ

Wind rushes past me
I close my eyes in pure love
Whoopsies! I just crashed!

KATHLEEN ALCALÁ is the author of five books as well as many stories and essays. Her work has received awards such as the Western States Book Award, the Governor's Writers Award, and two Artist Trust Fellowships. A resident of Bainbridge Island, she teaches creative writing at the Northwest Institute of Literary Arts.

Mora

ıılıןl!l!ıןınmılıןılıןll!ınlllllıןıןılllıןnnlıןılıןllııɪɪ!lıɪ

Just north of our neighborhood is a deep, wooded ravine that runs under the nearby highway to join a salmon stream. Just south are five acres of open land, privately owned. When I say open, I don't mean empty. The land is dense with salal, wild blackberries, and scrub trees. Our neighborhood, on a dead-end street, serves as a wildlife corridor between the two areas, one of the reasons we love it. On a regular basis, the neighbors sign petitions, write letters, and attend city council meetings to protect the Cave Avenue neighborhood from the encroachment of developers.

Our cat disappeared last week. This is not uncommon on Bainbridge Island, a few miles west of Seattle, but Pearl had lived with us for over fourteen years. She was a rescue cat from the county, and we figured her combination of caution and her ability to climb trees quickly had kept her safe.

It is the season for blackberries, and the bushes are especially prickly during this time, as though to give up the purple/black fruit to only the most worthy seekers. Right now deer, songbirds, crows, bluejays, raccoons, and yes, rats are feasting on the fruit. There is so much that many berries will simply fall, staining the road with their bloody juice. One summer evening I passed two Russian Orthodox priests in full regalia reaching to snatch berries from the closest vines, putting them directly into their mouths over their long white beards and pale albs, heedless of stains.

I waited a couple of days for the cat to turn up. After all, she is an indoor-outdoor cat, and although she tends to stick close to home, she is entitled to a little adventure. Only on the third day did I reluctantly put up 'Have You Seen Pearl?' posters around the neighborhood, feeling both worried and foolish. Maybe she was in somebody's garage.

The rugged nature of the vines means that, short of owning a moonsuit, it is impossible to enter either the ravine or the five acres to look for Pearl. Four days after her disappearance, several of us admitted that we could smell a rank odor by the side of the road. Narrowing it to a particular patch of berries, we returned with garden hoes. Gingerly, we pulled back the spiky vines, expecting to find the remains of our cat. Even with long sleeves and gloves we suffered bloody scratches and pricks. The vines, called *Rubus armeniacus,* are armed with a chemical irritant that keeps the scratches from healing quickly. The local common name for them is Himalayan blackberry, an invasive species along with Scotch broom and English ivy. There are work parties held on a regular basis to fight back the encroaching plants, especially where they climb trees or overrun the natural undergrowth around streams. No such work is ever done on these five acres.

Every summer, we take our colanders and gather berries. Entire families come from tamer neighborhoods, and the more industrious use footstools or stepladders to reach the fruit that hangs at a tantalizing distance, always just beyond arm's length. The plants I see sometimes reach six feet in height, and I think beyond that, their weight drags them down. The blackberry canes can reach out and grab you, soon entangling a foot or an arm in vicious thorns. Vine cutters or garden clippers are good tools to bring along. Blackberries can supposedly grow up to fifteen feet tall, with canes up to forty feet long.

The more ambitious harvesters pick buckets of berries to freeze and use over the winter months. They will bake cobblers, cookies, breads, and preserves. The grasshoppers among us will buy ice cream to accompany the fresh berries, living just for today. Or maybe sprinkle them on our cereal in the mornings. Here is a description from a local restaurant:

> For my money, there is no better dessert on Earth than the blackberry slump at the Four Swallows restaurant on Bainbridge Island, in Washington State. *Slump* doesn't sound all that appetizing to you? Fine; refuse to order it, as I did, and watch as it arrives in front of your tablemate smelling like home-baked memories and looking like a cake crossed with a crumble, with blackberries glistening like jewels amid vanilla ice cream and a toasty brown crust. When I finally persuaded my husband to share it, I discovered that the slump tastes even better than it looks. —*Amanda Allington, Honolulu, Hawaii*

The five acres are owned by a family descended from early white settlers on the island. Before that, it was part of the Hall Brothers Shipyard, along with our neighborhood. We sometimes find old bottles gone blue with age among the roots of the second-growth fir trees.

The island was part of the camping and fishing grounds of the Suquamish, Chief Sealth's people. They stuck to the beaches and left the dense, green interior to itself. A lot of ships were built from the first growth forest in the 1800s, making a few people very rich. Not a stick of old growth is left, although here and there are huge stumps attesting to their existence.

Salal, then invasive blackberries and ivy took over the spaces opened up to sunlight. With new meadows, and most predators killed or banished, the deer have proliferated. A doe and her two fawns move regularly through our yard, biting off rosebuds and nibbling the tender leaves of the hosta until my husband, infuriated, goes outside and throws rocks at them. They move on, hardly perturbed, to return the next night.

At dusk, the raccoons emerge, drinking from our birdbath and continuing on to the five acres to gorge. These raccoons are huge, easily twice the size of our seven pound cat. Still, they are not known to be aggressive unless cornered. Many times I have watched the cat and the raccoons look straight through each other. At first light, they will return to their nests in the ravine.

Three years ago, a family on the island opened an ice cream parlor offering fresh fruit flavors and interesting flavor combinations. "We churn old world flavors–Gianduja, Marron Glace and Dulce de Leche—that are traditional in our hometown, as well as new-school favorites—Goat Cheese with Fig, Banana Split and Lemon Bar," according to their website. This is a perfect business for Bainbridge, since we have many day visitors from Seattle, here mostly to ride the ferry roundtrip. You can't go wrong selling sweets to tourists. They named the business "Mora." Since the family was from Chile, I figured it was a family name. Recently, my son told me that it means blackberry. I had to stop and think, because I associated the word with a big tree from my childhood. We looked it up. Mora means blackberry or mulberry, but blackberry is listed first.

I knew only one grandparent, my father's mother, Refugio Ramirez Alcalá Gutierrez. A refugee from the Mexican Revolution, she owned a stone house in East Highlands, California, a short drive from our house in San Bernardino. She had transformed the property into a huge garden over the years, presided over by a spreading mulberry tree with big, dark green leaves. When I was in second grade, my class at school raised silk worms, and I supplied the voracious eaters with mulberry leaves, bringing useless bags of leaves even after they had spun their brown cocoons and transformed into frail moths.

I spent many hours in that yard, nibbling berries and pomegranates and other fruits that seem impossibly exotic to me now. I would invent kingdoms among the flower stalks and medicinal plants, build bug houses on a scale that made the adults look huge when I returned to them. It was a garden of earthly delights for a solitary child, while the joys and sorrows of an only son and his twice-widowed mother raged inside. It was mostly about money. Late in the afternoon, I would sit in the kitchen with my grandmother and drink tea with milk in it and eat graham crackers. That is what mora meant to me.

The rancid smell in the blackberries turned out to emanate from a rotting log that had probably attracted too much dog pee. We found no sign of Pearl. Later that day, unable to resist the abundance, we went farther down the road, away from the log, to gather berries for ourselves. Two days later, we consumed grilled salmon followed by blackberry pie at our neighbor's house. When Hilary lifted one of their indoor-only cats to her lap later that evening, I had to look away. A feeling of physical craving had come over me, the same I sometimes felt when I saw mothers with their young sons, still small enough to pick up. I missed my cat.

After two weeks, I stopped checking each door on a regular basis to see if the cat was waiting to be let in. I no longer call "Here kitty kitty, here Pearl," as I walk down the street. All but one poster of her, a compact gray tabby with a white bib and boots, has been taken down. No one called our number, or tried to collect the reward.

What I have avoided saying is this: Pearl was probably eaten by a coyote. She was snatched away in the dark sometime between 10:30 p.m., when I fell asleep, and 6:30 a.m., when she would normally enter the bedroom to see if anyone was willing to come downstairs and feed her.

My son, who came home over the weekend, does not seem too sad. He has been away at college for the better part of three years, accustomed to being absent from the cat, and us. People no longer tell us heroic cat stories of returns after a month, six months, a year. We have washed Pearl's blankets and brushed our chairs and couches. Her dishes have been put away, dismantling the miniature ecosystem in which a spider waited for tiny insects to visit her water dish. This might be a form of magical thinking, as Joan Didion would call it, that if we put her things away, Pearl will surprise us and return. But mostly, it just made me sad to see them.

The blackberries I eat with ice cream harbor a complicated flavor of sugars, fruit, and something darker, peaty, organic. It is a tangle of story lines, thousands of summers of growth and decay, the soaring song and the abrupt squeak. Somewhere in those brambles may lie Pearl's remains, already nurturing the growth of next season—sweet, and bitter.

Epistolary Tales

In our digital age, the art of physical letter writing is increasingly rare. But the students' writing in this section gives hope to the future of epistolary correspondence. In the first three pieces, students traveled to the Puget Sound Goat Rescue farm in Maple Valley for a summer writing workshop, then wrote letters back to their new four-legged friends— "Notes to Goats," from one kid to another.

Letters between human pen pals feature in this section too. One story comes from a student in the after-school Pen Pal Writing Club in which students write weekly letters back and forth with a senior pen pal living at the nearby University House Retirement Center. Students looked back on their correspondence for the year and mined their letters for real-life details, then used these details to write original fiction stories.

LUIS MARTINEZ is in fifth grade at Greenwood Elementary School. In addition to writing, he enjoys playing basketball, baseball, soccer, and clarinet.

Notes To Goats: Belle

Dear Belle,

Could you please tell Charlie for me that he was too excited to see me? So tell him next time, he should be more like you. You were amazingly calm. You were so calm that I thought you must be everybody's favorite. You're especially my favorite and you always will be. Barbara must be very lucky to have you. I would bet on that.

I know why you like to nibble on shirts, because it's kind of enjoyable. But I stopped doing it because my parents were mad. You know how parents are.

Sincerely,
Lou

MARIN CADY lives in Shoreline and is a fourth grader at Parkwood Elementary School.

Dear Charlie,

What are you doing right now? Are you eating? If you are eating, what are you eating? I learned you couldn't eat alfalfa. My brother, that was unfair; do you think so? I don't think so, because it might make you sick.

When you read this, I will be at Camp of the Cascades. I don't know what I will be doing at Camp of the Cascades, but I wish it had goats. It has horses, but they aren't the same. I will miss you and all the other goats at your farm.

When I was in your pen, I noticed you kept nibbling at my shirt. I don't know if that means you like me or if you just like nibbling on people's shirts. I hope it doesn't mean you *don't* like me, because I like you and I want you to be my goat-friend. I'm glad you didn't actually nibble a hole in my shirt. I would have been mad at you because it was my favorite shirt.

I also noticed that you didn't like it when I brushed your fur, but you liked it when someone else brushed you. But I wasn't jealous, so you don't have to worry, because I don't like it and think it hurts when I brush my own hair.

I learned a lot from you and really liked visiting your farm. I hope some day I'll be able to come back. I made two Japanese haiku poems for you:

Charlie is so nice
Charlie tried to eat my shirt
He nibbled at it.

Charlie is my friend
I hope to see Charlie soon
Charlie is silly.

From,
Marin

SARAH BELL is in sixth grade at Eckstein Middle School She loves animals, especially her guinea pig, and would like to visit Thailand, Japan, and Hawaii.

Notes to Goats: Tulip

Dear Tulip,

When I met you, I noticed that you were tan and white and very cute.

Do you like your hay? Or would you like to eat strawberries and raspberries and chocolate cake? I think you should try fruit and chocolate cake because I have had it and I fully recommend it (not saying that hay is bad or anything). I like how you were so friendly and happy when I patted you. I learned that you eat alfalfa, and the boys do not.

Best wishes,

Sarah

Terrific
Unique
Little
Inspiring
Playful

YONASE GELETA is a sixth grader at Seattle Academy of Arts and Sciences. In addition to being in the Pen Pal Writing Club, he is one of The Greater Seattle Bureau of Fearless Ideas' go-to students for readings, stage performances, and event MC-ing. Yonase and Jim have been pen pals for about one year.

Life Stories Over Pepperoni

It was 7 o'clock on a winter evening in Seattle. It was raining as usual. I, Jim Ward, had ordered a pepperoni pizza. The pizza delivery boy, Yonase, who was thirteen, came to University House to deliver it.

"Yonase! You're a pizza delivery guy?" I said.

"Maybe," Yonase said.

I looked in the box. "And half the pizza's gone?"

"Maybe," he said. "Let's not fuss about that right now. Tell me about your life."

"It was on this same day, December 14th, in 1944. I was eighteen and I was drafted into World War II. It changed my life dramatically, even to this day. I was miserable because I had to give up my whole life for war. I had a family and a very important girl. I met this girl when my family and I moved to Arizona from Detroit, Michigan. We moved because my dad got offered a new job in Arizona. On this day, December 14th, I was shipped to Palawan Island to fill in for the lost soldiers. I was okay with this move for a while because I had been training for months. No big deal, I thought, but it all changed.

"It was 3:04 a.m., and it was pitch dark. This day scared me for the rest of my life. You may ask why. Well, on that day all the troops and I walked straight into an ambush. I wasn't too scared until the guy right next to me, my good friend Bob, got shot in the earlobe. Bob always wanted to get his ears pierced but not this way. I mean, you can't get it pierced when your whole earlobe's shot off.

"The ambush started like this: there were bullets flying everywhere and grenades exploding at our feet. We were looking for safety and that's when the Philippine soldiers aimed at Bob and I. I ran for cover, but Bob was not fast enough. He aimed at them but he failed to get an accurate shot. That's when he tried to reload and was shot unexpectedly in the earlobe. I saw it all happen before my eyes, my best friend, my right hand man, was shot in the ear. To this day Bob is deaf."

"Wait, what happened with this 'important girl,' if you know what I mean?"

"Well, Yonase, I forgot to mention that through the course of this war we wrote non-stop to each other. I realized that I loved her. I was ready to go back home and marry her. In one of the letters, she told me that she loved me, I was surprised that she did because there were a lot of men back home in Arizona. I told her in the letter that if I make it out alive that we could be together and get married."

"What happened when you got home? Did you guys get married?"

"Yes, we did get married. We got married right away. We didn't want to waste any more time."

"Wait, is that Bob over there?"

"Yes, that is Bob."

"Wow, that's so cool that you're living with your best friend from war."

"Yeah, that is pretty cool."

"Thank you for telling me this amazing story about your life."

ROSS McMEEKIN's short fiction appears in *Shenandoah, Redivider, PANK, Hobart,* Tin House Flash Fiction Fridays, and elsewhere. He edits the literary journal *Spartan* and is a 2013-2014 Made at Hugo House Fellow. He was born and raised and now lives in Seattle.

Ice a Mile Thick

My son stares at the mazes of rusted, graffiti-scrawled pipes. He asks what they're for. The real answer is boring, so I say, "Scientific experiments on aliens."

"Someday I'm going to live here," he says.

The structure is actually a skeleton of an old gasworks factory that the city kept intact, for character, when they rezoned the area as a park. But my son's at that age where anything can happen, and I love borrowing that perspective when I'm with him. It's all the more special because I'm only allowed to be with him one weekend a month.

"I'm going to ask the aliens to build me a ship," he says.

"What kind?"

"Space," he says, like I'm stupid.

We climb the steep grass bank towards the top of the hill in the middle of the park. The hill we're climbing is carved with clusters of weird brass and stone markings, and at the top is a sundial. Like the pipes on the old factory, its design looks alien.

My son sees the sundial and I can tell he's imagining something wonderful. Then he looks back at me—and what's balanced on my shoulders—and remembers why we've come.

My neck is numb from carrying the block of ice all the way from the car. I'm glad to finally set it down and unwrap it from the plastic.

"So we slide on the ice?" he asks again.

He has already asked this five times in the last hour. He can't seem to understand when I explain it. "You'll see," I tell him.

Beyond our hill and the park are Lake Union and then the skyscrapers of downtown Seattle. Low floating clouds obscure the tops of a few of the taller ones.

"Twenty thousand years ago," I tell him, "this whole place was covered in a block of ice one mile thick."

"Why did it melt?" he asks, unfazed by the implications of the ice age. He's often excited about what I find mundane and bored with what I find fascinating. I think some of that's because he doesn't understand time well enough. Who really does, until too much has been spent? For my son, twenty thousand years is nothing, just three words representing a period that couldn't possibly be longer than his time-out this morning for dropping my cell phone into the fish tank. Whereas for me, twenty thousand years is awe-inspiring, a cold reminder of how little time we have.

"The ice all melted when the temperature warmed," I say.

He looks down at our block of ice. "Could it happen again?"

I prop my foot up on the block of ice. "Sure. We better hurry."

We take turns sliding. We scream through each descent. Then we run back up the hill and do it again. We do this over and over, sometimes together, sometimes alone, burning all the joy we can before the ice melts beneath us.

Afternoon slips into dusk. Rain clouds gather above us and spill. We look down; our ice block is now shaped like a comet. We both lean over, hands on our knees, trying to catch our breath, each waiting for the other to take the lead, neither wanting to continue but neither wanting to stop.

After a quick moment catching his breath, my son asks, "How much would it cost to live here?"

I want this question to imply that he wishes we could be together all the time, but another part of me wonders how and when he started worrying about cost. This is new. It's probably irrational, but I begin think about his mother and hope my payments are doing their job.

From there, I start to mull over if there's a way to broach the subject with his mother without offending her, which is its own sort of magical thinking. My stray words have already flooded most of the common ground we used to share.

"This neighborhood's pretty affordable," I lie.

"Good," he says. "Because we'll probably have to buy fuel for the spaceship."

"Can I come with you on the voyage?" I ask.

He thinks for a moment. "If Mom lets you," he says.

I look the other way, back towards Queen Anne hill, trying to hide my face from his eyes. He's said a mouthful; he has no idea how right he is about his mom. He has no idea why it's this way, and I plan on preserving his ignorance as long as possible. His ears will burn when he hears all I've put her through.

My son nudges me in the ribs with his elbow. "Look," he says.

And it starts. First there is just a glow coming from one of the old factory buildings. Then orange light begins to bleed and peel from the cracks and slivers between the pipes.

Slowly the entire building begins to split apart, like enormous jaws opening. We hear the whir of fans, the whistles of steam, the grinding of gears. The orange light—deep, like that of embers from a hearth—begins to pulse inside.

Then a huge, dull-grey pod, shaped like the comet our ice block has become, begins to rise. The whistling and grinding and whirring stops and we're left with just the hum of the hovering spacecraft and the sound of rain pinging against its frame.

Neither of us speaks. It's beautiful. I want to stay here forever.

But with a flash it's gone: the spaceship, the glow—everything.

We wait for a while in silence, but my son begins to shiver, so I pull him to his feet. I put my arm around his shoulder and we walk back down the hill. We leave what's left of the ice block to melt in the rain. There's no one else around; the park emptied when the showers arrived. The only sound now is rain smacking the grass and concrete.

The silence between us continues the whole way back through the park to my car, and the rest of the ride home to his mother's house. He won't say a word. Neither will I. It's like this every month; the last hour is the worst. To speak during that last stretch of time together feels like an offense. It's as though each second deserves a sacred attention, recognition, savoring, and to fill it with words might speed the loss of time.

When I pull up to his mother's house and turn off the car, he unbuckles his seatbelt and reaches over with both arms and gives me a hug. I try not to think about how soon he will be too old to hold on to me like this. Already he won't look me in the eyes when I drop him off. And he's long since stopped asking if I'm coming inside.

I bet in his imagination, I never left. I know I didn't in mine.

I Am, I Feel: Poetry in a New Language

Students in Carla Reynolds' class at Arts and Academics Academy, a public high school in the Highline School District, wrote a series of poems about identity. All the students were English Language Learners and recent immigrants to the United States. Their poems centered on the students' memories of their home countries, and their experiences as new residents in the United States. At the end of the project, the students' poems were published in a pocket-sized chapbook, *I Am, I Feel*. Finally, students did a public reading of their works, developing both written and spoken mastery of their new, second language.

ALBERTO SANCHEZ is from El Salvador and goes to Arts and Academics Academy High School in Highline.

Stadium Oscar Alberto in Santa Ana

The red and blue on fans,
Green grass, seats are red and blue
Ten people playing large drums with sticks
Everyone screaming and whistling for the whole team
I smell sweat on men's t-shirts swinging over their heads
I smell cigarette smoke and pomade
I watch people drinking cold water and beer
El Salvador stadium fans from little to big
My friends, Vladimir and Santo, and I remember watching,
Cheering, and whirling our t-shirts over our heads
I feel happy and excited when I remember my time with my friends.

ERICK CHAVEZ is from El Salvador. He goes to Arts and Academics
High School.

Costa del Sol

I dream about Costa del Sol
My favorite place
I think about the blue water,
The yellow sun, green palms,
The people swimming.
I remember the sound of the children laughing
The sound of the wind and the surf
I hear the seagulls crying
A happy, relaxed, feeling with the sun on my skin
The smell of salt fish and fresh air
The taste of sea water, ice cream, mango and fish
In El Salvador I remember the roses,
I remember the mountains and the beach
And so many animals:
Chameleons, parrots, monkeys, doves, hummingbirds and turtles
I remember swimming and playing soccer with my cousins Jonathan and Alex
I miss being with my aunt, Angela
I dream about being with my entire family from Seattle and El Salvador
All together on my favorite beach.

HOLMAN is from El Salvador. He goes to Arts and Academics Academy High School in Highline.

My Shoes

My shoes, red like blood
Running shoes made of leather, black laces.
Comfortable
Like an old chair.
Well-worn
Bought in a small store in Ilovasco, a year before I left.
Memories of my country, El Salvador.
Traveling to America in car, in bus, walking and running
My shoes, my journey.

TIEN DUONG is from Vietnam and goes to Arts and Academics Academy High School in Highline.

Grandmother's Necklace

Silver and diamond around my neck.
Miss my grandmother.
It symbolizes a love
She reserved for me.
She played and slept with me a long time ago.
I want to keep the necklace forever,
Until I give to my granddaughter.

VICTOR SANTAMARIA is from El Salvador and goes to Arts and
Academics Academy High School in Highline.

La Libertad

ᵖˡᵖˡᵖˡˡᵖᵢₙₙₙₗᵖˡᵖˡᵖˡˡₚᵢₗₗₗₗᵖˡᵖˡˡᵖˡᵖˡˡᵖᵢₙₙₙₗᵖˡᵖˡˡᵖᵢₗₗₗₗᵖˡˡ

It is a party
Happy and energetic
Like lifting weights
Or playing soccer

Waves like crumpled paper
Chirping and screeching of birds
The wash of conversations
The giant blender of music
Bachata, reggaeton, salsa, and merengue

On the coast of El Salvador during Easter week
Yellow-green grass and coconut trees
Stray dogs and cats running around
Playing soccer, swimming, and eating guisado chicken

Cream-colored sand, tiny crabs, and palm frond roofs
Is joyful, colorful, and relaxing
Flowery cologne, a rainbow of sweet drinks
I feel loved

LISH McBRIDE was raised by wolves in the Pacific Northwest. It rains a lot there, but she likes it anyway. She spent three years away while she got her MFA in fiction from the University of New Orleans, and she liked that too, although the hurricane Katrina did leave much of her stuff underwater. Her main goal in going to college was to become a writer so she could wear pajamas pretty much all the time. She currently resides in Seattle, spending most of her time at her day job at Third Place Books in Lake Forest Park. The rest of her time is divided between writing, reading, volunteering at The Greater Seattle Bureau of Fearless Ideas, and Twitter, where she either discusses her desire for a nap or her love for kittens. (Occasionally ponies.)

School of Fish

I woke up and I was a whale. Now, I know what you're thinking. Teenage girls—aren't they known for their exaggeration? Their hyperbole? Overly dramatic with their use of metaphor and whatnot. And while I may maintain a straight-A average in my English class and could certainly use those things appropriately, along with irony, sarcasm, and—thanks to Family and Consumer Sciences—a blowtorch, I wasn't doing so now.

No, when I say I woke up and I was a whale, I mean *I woke up in my bed and I was a black and white sea-going mammal.* At least I wasn't to proper scale. My tail hung over the foot of the bed, but I wasn't that much longer than I was the day before. Inches, maybe. I flicked my tail just to see it move. I hadn't gone to bed like this. I'm pretty sure I'd remember having skin like a hard-boiled egg and teeth that I could floss with a rope. Pity I was all done with the tooth fairy—my lower jaw alone could have put me through college. At least I was an orca and not something embarrassing like a beluga with its big domed head. Or worse, a sperm whale. There would be no living that one down.

So for a few minutes I just lay there, wondering what had happened and how I still managed to fit into my nightgown. Too bad it hadn't ripped—it was the itchy one my aunt gave me that Mom made me wear. If I'd busted the seams, I could have thrown it away.

Would Mom let me call in sick? Maybe. But it was the first day of school, and I didn't want to get behind. Besides this was going to be *my* year. I was going to enter high school a whole new Ellie. I'd run all summer and lost my baby fat. I'd traded most of my free nights for baby-sitting gigs and spent the money on a new wardrobe. New. Not hand-me-downs from my weirdo cousin, or worse, from my big brother. I'd traded my glasses for contacts and grown my hair out and spent the last of my money going to an actual salon. Grandma had two-inch lenses in her glasses and a shaky hand. She was *not* cutting my hair this year, no matter how much we saved doing it.

I'd done everything I could to set myself up for success. I didn't need to be the most popular person in school. I'm not greedy or delusional. I'd settle for mid-rung. If I could just make it through the year without Melanie and her friends snickering at me when I walked by, I'd be happy. I glanced down at my flippers, black and glossy despite being beached in my bed. All that work and I was an orca. Ugh.

My mom popped her head in the door. "You've got two minutes to get your butt out of bed and at the breakfast table, or you're on your own." I twitched my tail at her, but she didn't seem to notice. "I mean it, El. Two minutes."

Homemade breakfasts show up in my house with about the same consistency as Halley's Comet—like clockwork the first day of school and major holidays. Anything else was an anomaly. My mom is not the best or most avid cook, but it beat making my own breakfast, so I flopped onto the floor.

It's not the easiest thing to maneuver as an orca on land. They are creatures meant for the water, not a brown shag rug that had seen better days. My rug burn was going to be *stupendous*. I really wished I'd cleaned my room, or at least managed to get my dirty laundry into the hamper. Rolling around in last week's gym clothes was not my favorite thing I've ever done. Sadly, it's not the worst thing I've ever done, either. I felt pretty good when I finally managed to get to the breakfast table using a sort of wiggle/flipper push combo. The feeling was short-lived and left as soon as my mom yelled at me to get off the floor. I'd also taken too long and missed breakfast, so I'd have to make do with a freezer-burned toaster pastry.

My mom didn't seem too concerned about my new form. I wondered briefly if my brother would notice, but he'd fallen back to sleep at the table while waiting for the coffee to brew. He did Running Start at the college now, so he didn't have to ride the bus. In twenty minutes his best friend, who had a car, would pick him up for their carpool. Which I didn't think was fair. To skip high school *and* the bus? Lucky bum.

Getting dressed was a chore and a half. I ended up wearing a skirt and a sweater because it was the easiest thing to slip over my tail. I had to sort of dive into the sweater. It might only be September, but Seattle was doing its best to live up to its own hype with a cold, gray, rainy morning.

It took me ten minutes to adjust the straps on my backpack to account for my new shape, and even then it took some pulling and a good hard yank to get it in place. I'd almost decided to just carry it in my teeth by the end of it, I was so frustrated. By the time I'd managed, I'd missed the bus, and I had to beg a ride off my mom. At least I didn't have to worry about taking time to do my hair. Now that I'd had my first no-hair day, I was never going to complain about a bad hair day again. Or grandma's semi-dangerous bowl cuts. They hadn't been ranked fully dangerous yet because she'd only nicked me with the scissors. As soon as I lost an eye or a tip of an ear, we'd bump the status up.

My mom sighed as she filled up her travel mug. "One day in and you're already making me late for my commute. And I have a pre-meeting meeting to get ready for."

I didn't point out that if she'd left on time, she wouldn't have been here for me to beg a ride off her in the first place, or that preparing for a pre-meeting seemed to be against the idea of a pre-meeting to being with, but then again my mom's job didn't make much sense to me in the first place. I was smart enough to know that pointing out either wasn't the way to get her to do me a favor. It was a way to get grounded. Besides, if we started talking about her work, she might realize that I wasn't a hundred percent sure what she did for a living. Something in an office building with copy machines, meetings, and terrible coffee. I always zoned out when she talked about it.

"Fine," she said, pulling on her overcoat. "But you better be ready to walk out the door right now."

I tried to give her a thumbs up, but it ended up being more of a flipper wave.

"El, where on earth are your shoes?"

Since I couldn't quite figure out how to get my shoes on my new tail, I'd just planned on going bare foot...or I guess bare tailed? Clearly, though, my mom wasn't letting any child of hers out of this house looking like a homeless beggar. (Her words, not mine.) I stared at my black and white checkered rain boots. Then I stared at the graceful curve of my tail. How was I going to do this? Duct tape? Worried about chafing, I ended up perching the boots on the tapered ends and calling it a day. It looked ridiculous.

Mom dropped me off at the corner and I found an upside to my new condition: rain doesn't bother you when you're an aquatic-and-yet-suddenly-magically-land-based mammal. I waved my flipper at her as she drove away, then I kicked off my boots as soon as her car turned the corner. At this point I'd learned how to manage a pretty decent walk/hop, but I wasn't nearly as successful dragging my rain boots along.

The rain thing had me thinking. Maybe this wasn't so bad. Sure, I'd put in all that work this summer to lose the blubber only to gain it back and then some overnight, but I could salvage this. If I couldn't be popular for fitting in, maybe I could manage that weird level of notoriety where you do something so out of the norm that everyone at school seems to accept you on your own terms.

Like when that kid down the street created an app that told you if you had bad breath. (It worked on a scale from "minty fresh" to "killer halitosis.") He'd been a super tech nerd before that, but the fact that he'd succeeded so well with his app, and even made it into the online blog of the local paper, had pushed him into his own category. It was like he was able to make rules that applied just to him. Or like when Julie Ferrara broke her leg and wide leg jeans came back into style for a few months because she'd started wearing them. Could I do the same thing with my orca condition?

Thinking of this, my melon held high, I pushed my way through the double doors and into the hallway. The sight that greeted me brought me to a halt so abruptly, the kid behind me slammed into my backpack. The hallway was full of other sea creatures. Gray whales floated by, somehow unencumbered by their new state. It was like the hallways were their ocean—they just *fit*, you know? Which just figured since they were members of the football team.

A few of the drama otters raced down the hall, faces scrunched adorably as they talked and held their lunches to their chests. The librarian, Mr. Anderson, moved along the floor, pushed by strong ropy arms, the suction cups making little *poc-poc* noises. He made a stately octopus. Mr. Anderson nodded at me as he rolled by. Everyone seemed to have adapted to this new development better than me. No one was tripping over their own flippers or drooling out their blowhole.

Okay, so this wasn't so bad. If everyone else had gone through the same transformation as me, then I couldn't be called a freak, could I? After all, we were all in this together. We were all part of the same wonderful and strange ecosystem that was high school. Snout in the air and spine straight, I went to my locker.

I passed Melanie and her cronies, the unofficial queens of our school. They were all seals, except for poor Jenny, who'd become a sand shark. I wondered how long it would be until she was ostracized from the group for being different. Then again, maybe Melanie had mellowed with her transformation.

As I opened my locker, I heard it in Melanie's piping voice. "I can't believe she's an *orca*. How sad. Couldn't even manage something land-based. What a mutant. Still, I'm not surprised...."

I stopped listening, my cheeks burning. Could orcas blush? I hoped not. All of my time and sweat this summer, useless. Why would I think it even mattered? Even with this new playing field handed to us, they were still going to treat me like I was a bottom feeder. I stared at my feet, trying my best not to cry as a few of the guys scuttled by in their new Dungeness crab bodies. Matt gave me a nod and a "hey" and I managed a weak wave back.

This was stupid. I couldn't believe it. Anger and frustration burned through me. I wouldn't let them do this to me. I was an *orca*, for Pete's sake! Orcas are like the wolves of the sea—beautiful, majestic and deadly. They graced many a totem pole. Seattle loved orcas—we even named our mass transit system passes after them: Orca Card. There are no seal cards. In fact, who cared about seals anyway? All they did was lay around on the beach and eat stinky fish.

And that's when I remembered.

Orcas *eat* seals.

And all I'd had for breakfast was that tiny, tasteless, toaster pastry.

I smiled. Maybe this year wasn't a lost cause after all.

Camping for Beginners:
An Introduction to the Art of Survival

In July 2014, six students who are regulars in The Greater Seattle Bureau of Fearless Ideas' After School Tutoring program went on a camping trip to the Olympic Peninsula, to a twenty-five-acre organic farm near Quilcene, Washington, affectionately known as "Old Tarboo Farm."

The students traveled from Seattle by car and ferry. At the farm, they practiced pitching tents, hanging bear bags, and preparing for outdoor dining. They were also treated to a guided nature walk.

It was a magical weekend—a chance not only to observe wild salmon spawning grounds, hone their s'mores-making techniques, and play flashlight hide-and-go-seek—but also, as camper Rowan Murray put it, to "learn about nature and the world we live in."

Here are some of the things they experienced, and some sage advice from no-longer-newbie campers.

Campers take a break in the barn. Front row, from left Lilly Grey Rudge, Yonase Geleta and Edom Araya. Standing, Rowan Murray. Not pictured, campers Brook Geleta and Faiz Abdu, and camp counselors Alicia Craven, Susan Kostick, and Steve Siden.

Six-word Odes to Old Tarboo Farm

No wind, no rain, just sun – Lilly Grey Rudge

It hurt when I fell down – Brook Geleta

Flashlight, moonlight, hide and seek camping – Steve Siden

Cool morning, deep dew, cock-a-doodle-doo, Tarboo – Susan Kostick

I love Tarboo, it is cool – Edom Araya

Verdant beauty, boundless hilarity, new tradition – Alicia Craven

Tarboo is the best place ever – Yonase Geleta

A Dozen Wise Camping Tips

1. Don't die.
2. Bring a flashlight.
3. Go with good friends who have been camping before.
4. Use bug spray.
5. Don't touch and eat adult stinging nettles.
6. Don't knock down another camper's hot dog, bad things happen.
7. Don't eat five biscuits no matter how small, you will regret it!
8. Use a camping pad.
9. Watch out for dew and doo doo.
10. Don't set a charred stick on the grass, fire occurs.
11. Sound carries through tent walls.
12. Never go where the pokey plants are.

When Camping, Some Sensory Experiences You Might Have

- Many flies got on me.
- I touched a hen.
- Hearing boys talk to each other.
- Roosters at 5 a.m.
- Seeing a beaver scent mound by the stream.
- Tasting a thimble berry.

Fond Camping Memories to Take Home

- I saw geese.
- I run as fast as I can, looking for a hiding place. We are playing hide and seek at night. I dive behind a tree, only to be found.
- Eating red huckleberries while on a nature walk.
- Hiding with Edom by the garden while Lilly Grey looked for everyone singing the "Striped Sweater" song.
- Faiz's whispered advice by the campfire: "Just sit back and watch the stars—it's amazing."
- I found a real live cow.
- Hiding really well.

PETER MOUNTFORD's debut novel, *A Young Man's Guide to Late Capitalism* (Houghton Mifflin) won the 2012 Washington State Book Award. His second novel *The Dismal Science* was published in 2014 by Tin House Books, and was named a *New York Times* Editor's Choice. His work has appeared in *The Atlantic Monthly*, *The New York Times Magazine*, *Southern Review*, *Granta*, *Slate*, *Best New American Voices 2008*, *Boston Review*, and elsewhere. He teaches at Sierra Nevada's low-residency MFA, and is the events curator at Hugo House, a place for writers in Seattle.

Sailing the High Seas of Book Piracy

I wouldn't have known about my Russian pirate translator had I not set a Google alert for the title of my debut novel when it was initially published in 2011. Over the following year, the alerts had inevitably, depressingly become more infrequent. Worse still, they began to occasionally refer to eBay sales (*Like New! Unread!*). The title, *A Young Man's Guide to Late Capitalism*, began to seem freshly ironic, given the circumstances.

But in March, 2012, the alerts began pointing me to a message board on the online forum WordReference. There, a user with the handle AlexanderIII was regularly seeking help understanding my unusual word choices. He wanted to know, for example, what I had meant when I described the interior of a Bolivian hotel with mid-1970s decor as having "cucumber walls." He wondered if that might mean that the walls had the *texture* of a cucumber, or maybe, he offered inexplicably, it meant that the walls were paisley.

Fortunately, se16teddy, a user with a teddy bear avatar, cleared things up:

se16teddy: I don't associate the paisley pattern with cucumbers at all. I suppose it must be the colour: it is quite common to describe colours in terms of a familiar fruit (orange, peach, plum, apple, aubergine …)

Two days earlier, AlexanderIII had been perplexed when I described my protagonist as waking up with his "hair askew, eyes puffy with sleep…" Did "hair askew" refer to a hairstyle, he wanted to know, or did he just have bed head? A user with the handle *Copyright*—of all things!—assured him the hair was askew as a result of sleep.

At first, I didn't realize that AlexanderIII was translating the book; I thought he was just a fastidious Russian reader with a loose command of the English language. It was fun to see people—even kooky message-board lurkers—debating the meaning of my thoroughly worked-over phrases.

After a few days, a member named DocPenfro encouraged AlexanderIII to simply enjoy the book and not fret over all the details. To which AlexanderIII responded: "I'd love to, DocPenfro, but I'm translating it for a publisher so I must be sure."

Holy crap, I thought, *my book is going to be published in Russia!* Then I remembered that no Russian publisher had acquired the rights. That was when it finally dawned on me that AlexanderIII must be translating it for some kind of book-pirating outfit.

In the U.S., book piracy of any kind is almost unheard of. But Russia, it turns out, has a remarkably mature black market for literature—particularly for e-books. Apparently, Russians love e-books. And that's where the piracy action is at, no doubt in part because the overhead is so much lower (no paper, no factory, no warehouse, no shipping, etc.). According to Rospechat, the Russian state agency that regulates mass media, 90 percent of e-book downloads are illegal, and these pirate sales amount to several billion rubles a year. Black-market e-books are not just cheaper—they're more plentiful. Rospechat estimates that Russians have access to more than 100,000 pirated titles, compared to just 60,000 legitimate titles. Not surprisingly, lawful Russian publishers are being crushed by the illicit market.

Of course, I wish one of Russia's two major publishers had given me a couple thousand dollars for the Russian rights, but they didn't. Like many novelists I know, I'm just happy to have someone reading my work, whether or not they're paying for it.

Also, I find it heartening that Russians care enough about reading to sustain a robust literary black market. In the U.S., you get the feeling that no one is pirating e-books because—well, who'd buy such a thing?

I considered contacting AlexanderIII to offer translation help, but I sensed that if I wrote to him, he might vanish. He might even stop translating the book. So I became a voyeur to my book's own abduction, and—confusingly—I found myself rooting for the abductor.

Though I was impressed by AlexanderIII's dedication, I'm sorry to say that his numerous message-board queries did not inspire much confidence in his command of the English language. At one point, he indicated that he was struggling with "white liberal guilt."

Me too! I wanted to chime in, but I held back.

He postulated that white liberal guilt meant: "the guilt for consuming white substance (cocaine)."

This query spurred a cavalcade of responses from eloquent and cheerful fluent English speakers, who for some reason haunt the message board offering advice to Russian literary pirates. In this case, Gwan rushed in to explain that white liberal guilt indicates "that they are white (of European descent) men/women in a country colonised by Europeans."

AlexanderIII, apparently satisfied by Gwan's definition, dropped the matter, but I wondered what he thought about this idea of white liberal guilt, which seems the loftiest of all first world problems. If he was amused by such a notion, he didn't say so.

The rest of AlexanderIII's posts were likewise met with a barrage of advice from jovial English speakers who'd invoke definitions from the OED, conjecturing about what the author really meant when, say, describing Bolivian street kids "zooted on shoe polish."

AlexanderIII: Does this mean the kids had smoked marijuana before shining shoes?

PaulQ: As you can see from the context, it is highly unlikely that the shoeshine boys would be smoking marijuana on boot polish. From Urbandictionary.com = Zooted: "being so high the only words you can say are daang im zooted."
Shoe polish can be melted to provide a drink (?) that will have strongly intoxicating effects. It is usually drunk by severe alcoholics or others too poor to afford proprietary alcohol, beer/wine/spirits/etc. (Do not try this at home.)

AlexanderIII: I see. Thank you very much, PaulQ. I've checked Urbandictionary but somehow have not found about drinking the melted shoe polish. This seems to suit best.

At that point, I very nearly intervened to prevent any of my Russian readers from inviting severe injury or death. The *lustrabotas*, or Bolivian shoe-shine kids, get high from *huffing* polish, not drinking it. Before I could burst in to clear this chaos up, cyberpedant came to the rescue:

cyberpedant: Drinking melted shoe polish??? This seems absolutely incomprehensible. Sniffing it is far more likely, as the volatile chemicals are far more easily (and effectively) ingested through the nose. But, "whatever rings your chimes."

In April, a few weeks into his work, AlexanderIII unceremoniously dropped my novel and began translating Denis Lehane's *Gone, Baby, Gone*. I was shattered. Even my pirate translator had lost interest in my book. But in early July, my Google alerts informed me that AlexanderIII had dropped Lehane and returned to the good stuff.

At one point in the novel, I'd described my protagonist's mother has having a "... sentiment born of her cloying, overly maternal side." AlexanderIII hypothesized that I had meant "...a sentiment born of her memory about hardships of solitary life." Despite being completely off base, AlexanderIII was drilling toward the character's deeper psychological core. I loved that. He completely misread the text, but he was wrestling with the sentences much as I had wrestled with them originally, laboring over the nuances and implications.

And so it was that, in early July, I finally wrote to AlexanderIII:

Me: I've noticed that you have many questions about [*A Young Man's Guide to Late Capitalism*] for the Russian translation that you're working on. As the author of the book, I am uniquely qualified to help you with these questions. Would you like my help?

No answer. He immediately stopped posting on the board. Then, a couple weeks later, to my surprise, AlexanderIII wrote to me. It's crazy to help someone steal my work, I know, but I couldn't help striking up a tenuous partnership with him. I still don't know who exactly he's working for, and no one has sought to acquire Russian rights to my novel. Even so, I wish I could understand his translation: I'd love to know what book he was reading.

Additional Contributors

David Rzegocki is a freelance photographer and elementary Spanish teacher based in Seattle. He began taking pictures while living abroad in Spain and has continued his work as a photojournalist and wedding photographer working around the Pacific Northwest and abroad. David enjoys taking pictures of people and telling visually striking stories through images. See his photograph in "Loose in the Kitchen" in this book.

Megan Wittenberg was born and raised in Seattle. After studying many subjects in art and biology, she finally found her place in the Scientific Illustration Program at the University of Washington. Combining a sense of design and beauty with her love of detail and accuracy brings her joy. Megan's work is published in many publications, including the books *The Wild Plants of Greater Seattle* and *The Maritime Northwest Garden Guide*. See her field sketch in "The Stone" in this book.

Acknowledgements

The Greater Seattle Bureau of Fearless Ideas would like to thank these fearless people for their invaluable support of this book.

PRODUCTION TEAM
Alicia Craven, Teri Hein, Sue Spang, and Bill Thorness.

ADULT AUTHORS AND ARTISTS
Kathleen Alcalá, Chelsea Cain, Megan Kelso, Margot Kenly, Lish McBride, Ross Mc-Meekin, Jessica Mooney, Peter Mountford, Tom Robbins, David Rzegocki, Jennie Shortridge, Matthew Simmons, Jess Walter, David B. Williams, and Megan Wittenberg.

STUDENT AUTHORS
Abdulahi Abdi, Faiz Abdu, Yusuf Ali-Halane, Edom Araya, Sophia Baldwin, Frances Baker, Sarah Bell, Marin Cady, Gerardo Cervantes-Naranjo, Erick Chavez, Alyson Chew, Deangelos "DJ" Clark, Jessica Darlington, Sadie Dokken, Tien Duong, Brook Geleta, Yonase Geleta, Holman, Eric Luna, Kyle Marston, Luis Martinez, Rowan Murray, Zoe Newton, Miles Rappaport, Gin Ronco, Silas Ronco, Lilly Grey Rudge, Alberto Sanchez, Victor Santamaria-Velasco, Arcadia Seilestad Helen Seretse, Jennaka Taton, and Max Tran.

YOUTH ADVISORY BOARD MEMBERS
Melat Assefa, Finn Colando, Brook Geleta, Laura Malatos, Haddy Njie, Cece Roseman, Jasmine Sun, and Sam Zagula.

WORKSHOP LEADERS AND ADULT EDITORIAL BOARD MEMBERS
Kathleen Alcalá, Justin Allan-Spencer, Rebecca Brinson, Diana Bryant, Megan Burbank, Alex Halsey, Alison Jennings, Sam Hernandez, Barbara Jamison, Susan Kostick, Jared Leising, Joely Mork, Forrest Perrine, Kate Pluth, Lana Sanderson, Dan Shumow, Steve Siden, Andrew Simon, Stephanie Wilson-Rothfuss, Miles Wray, and Steve Yasukawa.

IN-SCHOOLS PROGRAMS TEACHERS

Angie Armbrust, Viewlands Elementary
Nohra Giraldo, Proyecto Saber at Ballard High School
Debbie Spiegelman, Proyecto Saber at Ballard High School
Carla Reynolds, Arts and Academy High School
Jessie Towbin, Big Picture Middle School

BOOK DESIGNER

Tony Ong

EDITOR AND PROJECT MANAGER

Bill Thorness

THE GREATER SEATTLE BUREAU OF FEARLESS IDEAS STAFF

Justin Allan-Spencer, Humaira Barlas, Alaina Buzas, Joe Concannon, Alicia Craven, Teri Hein, Peggy Allen Jackson, Larisa Lumba, Brooke Matson, Leslie McCallum, Sean Palmer, Sue Spang, and Travis Thompson.

HOTEL PARTNERS

Hyatt Grand
Hyatt at Olive 8
Madison Renaissance
Cedarbrook Lodge
Washington Athletic Club - Inn at the WAC

GREENWOOD SPACE TRAVEL SUPPLY CO

The Greenwood Space Travel Supply Company is this planet's foremost purveyor of space travel supplies. Before embarking on your next interplanetary trip, visit our flagship store located at 8414 Greenwood Avenue North in Seattle's Greenwood neighborhood. If you are like many travelers and prefer the all-hours convenience of cyberspace, please direct your web browser to:

www.greenwoodspacetravelsupply.com

All proceeds from this book and the retail store benefit the work of The Greater Seattle Bureau of Fearless Ideas, a 501(c)3 non-profit writing and communication center for the students of Earth.